DEBORAH CLARK

WILDFLOWERS OF UTAH'S COLORADO PLATEAU

A FIELD GUIDE TO WILDFLOWERS OF CAPITOL REEF NATIONAL PARK AND SURROUNDING AREAS OF SOUTHERN UTAH

trails books
AN IMPRINT OF BOWER HOUSE
DENVER

Designed by Margaret McCullough
Layout by Sonya Unrein
Photography thanks to Thomas O. Clark
Illustration thanks to Patricia Hansen (the artist retains all copyrights)
Back cover image: View to Factory Butte from atop North Caineville Mesa, Utah

Printed in the Canada

Library of Congress Control Number: 2021932088
ISBN 978-1-934553-80-0

10 9 8 7 6 5 4 3 2 1

A Cautionary Note: Ingesting or touching wild plants or plant parts can pose a potential extreme health risk that could result in illness or even death. No one should attempt to make use of any wild plant for food or medicinal purposes based on the information provided in this book. The author, publisher, and all others associated with the production and distribution of this book assume no liability for the actions of the reader.

DEDICATION

I would like to dedicate this book to the memory of my father, Charles Hansen, who started taking me out in the field at a very young age, sharing his love and knowledge of native plants and wildlife with me. He was a wildlife biologist for the US Fish and Wildlife Service and the National Park Service, so I grew up in remote locations surrounded by nature. By the time I was seven years old, I remember going on trips with him and learning to identify and remember scientific names of shrubs and wildflowers in the Mojave Desert where we lived.

ACKNOWLEDGMENTS

This effort was a work in progress for many years. It's completion was achieved through the support, assistance and encouragement of friends and family. I would like to specifically thank my husband for his continual support and companionship on our many wildflower identification and photographic trips. My mother deserves special recognition for the innumerable hours she spent sitting on a stool in the field and bent over a desk sketching and inking the drawings to make this book a special family effort. Fred Goodsell and Keith Durfey took me on innumerable hikes and horseback rides in Capitol Reef National Park showing me new locations, quizzing me on plant names, and encouraging me to continue this project. Both of these gentlemen have passed away before seeing this edition, however, their assistance and friendship will always be remembered for making this book possible. Christine Groebner joined my husband and I on many botany field trips, helping to identify and of course, enjoy the wildflowers. Shirley Torgerson and Diana Elmer offered many good ideas and support throughout the project. Thank you to everyone who has helped keep me progressing forward on this project.

TABLE OF CONTENTS

(left) Eastwood's Indian Paintbrush *Castilleja scabrida*

INTRODUCTION

This new edition of *Wildflowers of Utah's Colorado Plateau* has been expanded beyond species found in Capitol Reef National Park to include over two hundred plants growing throughout Utah's Colorado Plateau, areas to which many of the species included in this book are endemic. This covered territory includes Southern Utah's National Parks: Arches, Canyonlands, Bryce Canyon, Capitol Reef, and Zion; National Monuments: Cedar Breaks, Bears Ears, and Natural Bridges; and Glen Canyon Recreation Area.

Entries for each species in this book will refer to the locations where they occur, mostly in Southern Utah but will also reference places where they might grow elsewhere in the United States. This book includes about fifty endemic species not included in other Colorado Plateau wildflower field guides.

Southern Utah parks and monuments draw millions of people each year, primarily because of diverse geologic formations and features. The canyons, cliffs, rock formations, and hoodoos are notable for their vibrant colors and shapes, and they depict the diverse geology of each area. The wide range of exposed geologic formations creates a great diversity of soil types for plants. Additionally, canyons created by wind and water erosion create a plethora of environmental niches for plants.

Among these locations, Capitol Reef National Park is extraordinary. At approximately 241,900 acres, Capitol Reef was established to protect the longest exposed monocline in North America. This wrinkle in the earth's crust runs about one hundred miles north to south and is named the Waterpocket Fold. There are seventeen geological formations exposed within the Fold, each combining different minerals, soil types, water moisture, aspect, and slope. Elevations of the Fold range from over 11,000 feet at the northwest to around 4,000 feet in the south at Halls Creek. This diverse range of elevations in combination with differences in precipitation and exposed geology allows for the evolution of endemic plant species. Many of these species have limited distributions and occur only in a specific geologic formation, aspect, or elevation range.

(left) Constance's Phacelia *Phacelia constancei*

There are over forty rare and endemic plant species, eight of which are federally listed, that occur in the Waterpocket Fold.

The other parks and monuments contain several of the same geologic formations (see Figures 1a and 1b) as Capitol Reef and they overlap Capitol Reef's elevational range, however none contain the same combination of both diverse geology and wide elevational range.

Glen Canyon National Recreation Area contains the oldest visible geologic formation, the Paradox Formation, from the Permian Period (formed about 300 million years ago). It also encompasses the lowest elevations of these management areas, about three thousand feet at its lowest point. Glen Canyon and Canyonlands National Park contain the most exposed geologic formations, twenty-one and twenty-two respectively. The Recreation Area also encompasses lands with an elevational range of over 4,500 feet from the lowest to the highest point, making it a close match to Capitol Reef in overall diversity.

Zion National Park contains a 5,000-foot elevational range but it encompasses only nine exposed geologic formations. Similarly, Bears Ears National Monument ranges from 9,000 feet down to a bit over 4,000 feet in elevation and encompasses only four geological formations. To the northeast, Canyonlands has the greatest spread of visible formations across time, ranging from the Honaker Trail formation, from the Permian Period, to the Claron and Green River formations formed about 65 million years ago during the Cretaceous Period. But all this geologic history is encompassed within an elevational range of only about 3,500 feet. Nearby, Arches National Park has some of the same geologic formations visible, however its elevational range is only about 1,500 feet.

Bryce Canyon National Park and Cedar Breaks, with their fabulous hoodoo features, represent the most recent formations of this suite of parks and monuments. Some Navajo Sandstone, from the Jurassic Period, can be seen in Bryce Canyon, but most of the formations in Bryce Canyon and Cedar Breaks are from the Cretaceous Period (145 to 65 million years ago). Among these locations, Cedar Breaks National Monument contains landscapes above ten thousand feet. This combination of diverse geology, soil types, aspect, and elevational differences explain why these parks and monuments contain so many plant species, many of which are endemic to Southern Utah.

VISITOR IMPACT

Southern Utah's parks, monuments, and the recreation area are primarily backcountry areas that receive millions of visitors each year. Many of these visitors hike the trails and backcountry that have rare plant populations within or adjacent to them. It is against National Park Service, Forest Service, and Bureau of Land Management regulations for anyone to pick any plant or plant part while exploring these areas. Since there are so many rare endemic species in Southern Utah, it is imperative that visitors not collect plants. By leaving the plants intact, you will help ensure that future generations can experience the diverse variety of wildflowers in Southern Utah. As always, photographs are a wonderful way to help identify, remember, and enjoy wildflowers.

IDENTIFYING SPECIES USING THE GUIDEBOOK

The book is organized by flower color, then arranged alphabetically by the plant's family and scientific names. *Family name* is noted at the beginning of each species description for readers who are knowledgeable about plant families. *Scientific names* are standardized and follow Intermountain biota (2019). The common names of plants are not standardized, and some plants have more than one common name. I have used common names that are well known in this area, but it is possible that alternate names may be used more frequently in different regions.

To identify a wildflower or shrub, turn to the section that corresponds to the predominant color of that flower. Several plants have flowers that are more than one color or are different colors in different locations due to genetic variation. If you can't find the wildflower you are looking for in one color section, turn to the next most likely color using the following guidelines:

- A flower may often be white or cream in some populations and bluish, yellow, or pink in another.
- If the plant you are looking for does not appear in the section of your first color choice, check the white to cream-colored flower section.
- For difficult colors, flower shape can be your guide.
- Occasionally, fruits can be helpful distinguishing features, so some of the drawings or photographs depict seedpods or fruit rather than—or in addition to—the flower.
- Always look for unique features of any flower, seed, or leaf to help with identification.

Each species covered here has a brief written **description** that provides identifying characteristics, flowering period, species range, habitat, and elevation range.

The flowering period reported is for blooming times for these species in Southern Utah, but the species may bloom longer or at slightly different time periods in other locations. Underlined words are technical terms and are defined in the **Glossary**. The **Comments** section provides information on historic or medicinal uses of a species, the derivation of its scientific name, locations where the species can be found, and its rarity, if applicable. The **Selected References** section provides a list of books for those interested in learning more about a species or how it has been used by Native Americans or pioneers.

Occasionally, comparison to similar species is noted in the **Comments** section. Since over 2,500 plant species occur in the Southern Utah region, closely related species may be mentioned but not covered in this guidebook. For species that are not covered, you may be able to identify them to family or genus with the information here and then seek out additional information from technical books, some of which are listed in the **Selected References**.

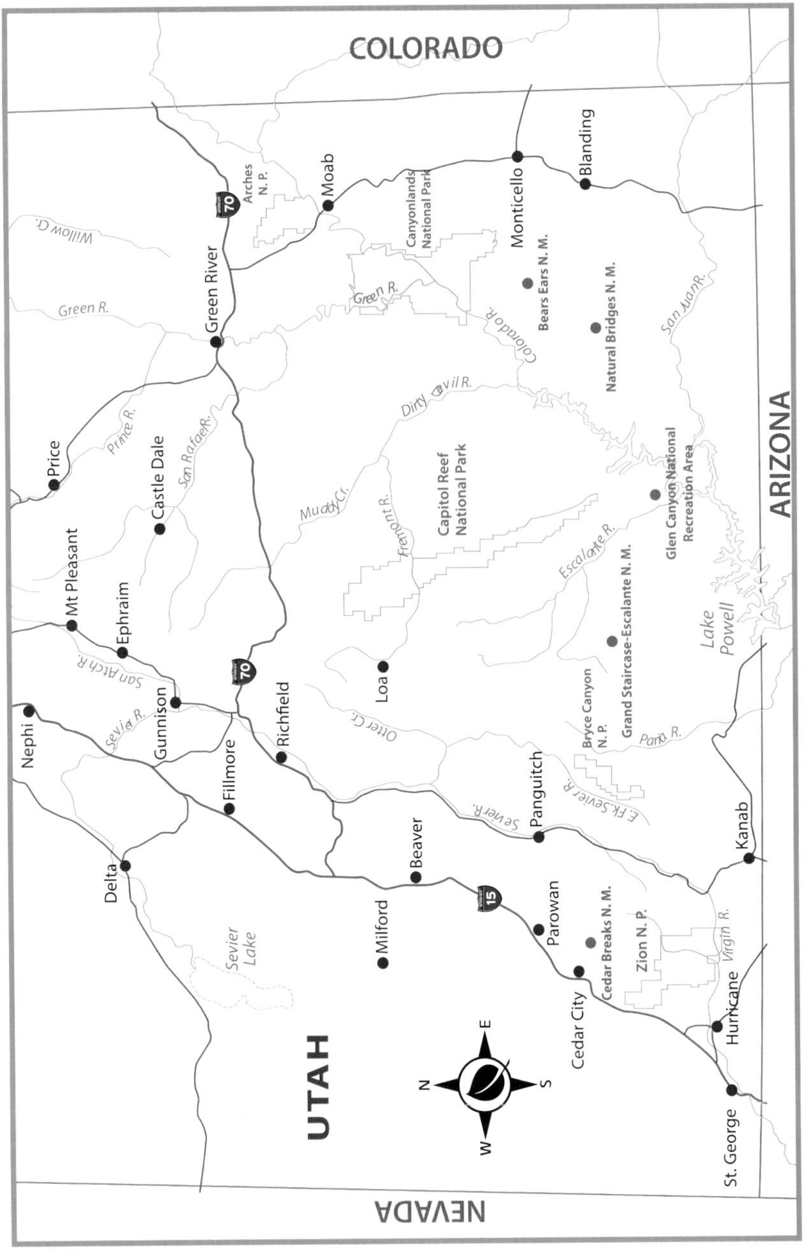

COLORADO
ARIZONA
NEVADA
UTAH
Arches N. P.
Moab
Canyonlands National Park
Monticello
Blanding
Willow Cr.
Green River
Green R.
Bears Ears N. M.
Natural Bridges N. M.
San Juan R.
Colorado R.
Dirty Devil R.
Price
Prince R.
San Rafael R.
Castle Dale
Capitol Reef National Park
Glen Canyon National Recreation Area
Muddy Cr.
Fremont R.
Escalante R.
Mt Pleasant
Ephraim
San Pitch R.
Gunnison
Sevier R.
Nephi
Richfield
Loa
Otter Cr.
Grand Staircase-Escalante N. M.
Bryce Canyon N. P.
Paria R.
Lake Powell
Fillmore
Panguitch
E. Fk. Sevier R.
Kanab
Delta
Beaver
Milford
Parowan
Cedar Breaks N. M.
Zion N. P.
Virgin R.
Sevier Lake
Cedar City
Hurricane
St. George
70
15
N
E
S
W

Time Frame	Period	Formation	Canyonlands NP	Glen Canyon NRA	Capitol Reef NP	Arches NP	Natural Bridges / Bears Ears NM	Zion NP	Bryce Canyon NP	Cedar Breaks NM
145.5 - 65.5 mya	Cretaceous	Sevier River							X	
		Green River	X							
		Brian Head								X
		Claron	X						X	X
		Mesa Verde	X		X					
		Kaiparowits							X	X
		Wahweap							X	X
		Straight Cliffs		X					X	X
		Tropic Shale		X					X	
		Mancos Shale	X		X	X				
		Dakota Sandstone	X	X	X	X			X	
		Cedar Mountain	X		X	X				
201.6 145.5 mya	Jurassic	Morrison	X	X	X	X				
		Summerville	X		X					
		Curtis	X		X	X				
		Entrada	X	X	X	X			X	
		Carmel	X	X	X	X		X	X	
		Temple Cap						X		
		Page		X	X					
		Navajo	X	X	X	X	X	X	X	

Figure 1a Geologic time frame and exposed formations in southern Utah's national parks and monuments.

Time Frame	Period	Formation	Canyonlands NP	Glen Canyon NRA	Capitol Reef NP	Arches NP	Natural Bridges / Bears Ears NM	Zion NP	Bryce Canyon NP	Cedar Breaks NM
251 - 201.6 mya	Triassic	Kayenta	X	X	X	X	X	X		
		Springdale Sandstone						X		
		Moenave		X				X		
		Wingate	X	X	X	X	X			
		Chinle	X	X	X	X		X		
		Shinarump (Chinle)								
		Moenkopi	X	X	X	X		X		
299 - 251 mya	Permian	Cutler	X		X					
		White Rim	X	X						
		Organ Rock	X	X						
		Kaibab Limestone		X	X			X		
		Cedar Mesa	X	X			X		X	
		Elephant Canyon		X						
		Halgaito Shale / Lower Cutler	X	X						
		Honaker Trail	X	X						
		Paradox		X						

Figure 1b Geologic time frame and exposed formations in southern Utah's national parks and monuments.

WHITE TO CREAM FLOWERS

WIDEWING SPRING PARSLEY

Cymopterus purpurascens | **Carrot Family** Apiaceae

A blue-green herbaceous perennial that is 2" to 6" tall. Plant appears more flattened on the ground rather than erect and upright. Foliage is covered with a whitish to bluish waxy coating giving the plant its blue green color. Plant base tends to be covered with dried, old brownish leaf bases. **Leaves** are primarily basal. Leaves (including the leaf stalk) are up to 5" long, are two to three times pinnately compound with three to six opposite pairs of lateral leaflets. The leaflets are oblong to ovate in shape, ¼" to 1" long (terminal leaflets are reduced), and ⅛" wide. Flowering stalk is usually 3½" tall. Whitish **flowers** occur in a flat-topped cluster with one to three clusters per stem. Flowers have a greenish purplish mid-vein extending up the petal lobes. **Fruit** is about ½" long, oblong in shape with wings. **Blooms** March to June. **Occurs** throughout Utah to Idaho, California, and New Mexico. Found in desert scrub, sagebrush, pinyon juniper, and ponderosa pine communities. (3,500 to 9,000 ft)

COMMENTS: Found throughout Capitol Reef. Most commonly seen along the Cathedral Valley Loop drive in early spring. It also occurs in Arches, Bears Ears, and Glen Canyon. *Cymopterus* is the Greek word for wavy wing, referring to the margins of its winged fruits. American Indians used the taproot and leaves as food. They also used the leaves of some species in this genus as seasonings and a mouth freshener.

Synonyms: Cymopterus montanus var. purpurascens

POISON MILKWEED

Asclepias labriformis | **Dogbane Family** Apocynaceae

An erect, herbaceous perennial up to 20" tall. Narrow, pale green **leaves** are 2" to 6" long and about 1" wide and occur irregularly along the stem. **Stems** and leaves are smooth and free of hairs. Pale cream to greenish **flowers** less than ½" in size bloom from the upper tips of stems; the tiny hoods appear flattened, or cut off, rather than tapered at the ends. **Seed** capsules are broadly spindle shaped, hang down along the stem, and are 1½" to 2¾" long and up to 1¼" wide with smooth surfaces. **Blooms** May to July. **Occurs** only in Utah, primarily in the eastern part of the state. It grows primarily in fine sandy soils in washes or canyons in desert scrub and pinyon juniper communities. (5,000 to 7,600 ft)

COMMENTS: The type locality is in Capitol Wash that runs through Capitol Reef. This endemic species is not common, but can be seen in appropriate habitats in Capitol Reef and Canyonlands National Parks. It is deadly, requiring only minute amounts of the plant to cause death in livestock, and should be considered extremely poisonous to humans.

FUNNEL LILY

Androstephium breviflorum | **Asparagus Family** Asparagaceae

A small perennial that grows from an underground bulb. The plant has one to three grass-like **leaves** that sprawl on the ground. These leaves are typically five-veined. Three to eight white to greenish **flowers** are borne on a naked stalk. They are funnel shaped, about ¼" wide with purple veining lengthwise along the petals. Three lobed **seed** capsules (about ½" long and equally wide) are filled with tiny black seeds. **Blooms** April to July. **Occurs** throughout Utah, to Colorado, Nevada, and Arizona. Found in fine textured clay or saline soils in saltbush, blackbrush, sagebrush, and pinyon juniper communities. (2,700 to 6,500 ft)

COMMENTS: Typically seen in the lower elevations at the southern end of Capitol Reef, and in Arches, Canyonlands, Bears Ears, Glen Canyon, and Zion.

Synonyms: Brodiaea paysonii

SAND LILY

Eremocrinum albomarginatum | **Asparagus Family** Asparagaceae

An erect lily reaching 14" tall. Basal **leaves** are linear, often nearly as long as the plant is tall; they may be erect or spread out on the ground. **Flowers** grow along a stalk, are about ⅔" across, whitish with greenish patches on the petals. Seeds are tiny and black. **Blooms** April to June. **Occurs** in south central Utah and northern Arizona. Found in sandy soils and often sand dunes in blackbrush, mixed desert scrub, and desert grasslands. (3,700 to 6,200 ft)

COMMENTS: This Colorado Plateau endemic is found in the southern portions of Capitol Reef and east near Hanksville. It also occurs in Arches, Canyonlands, Bears Ears, and Glen Canyon.

HARRIMAN'S YUCCA

Yucca harrimaniae | **Asparagus Family** Asparagaceae

A perennial with stiff, long, narrow, pointed leaves that grow in single or numerous rosettes around a central stalk. Plant can reach 20" tall. **Leaves** are curved in cross section such that they are concave on one side and convex on the other side. When leaves are old they often have white fibers peeling away from leaf margins. The flower stalk reaches 30" in height with broad, bell shaped yellow to cream **flowers** surrounding the stalk. Flowers are 1½" to 2" long and may be tinged with purple. **Seeds** are fairly large, cylindrical in shape with a pointed tip that flares open when mature. **Blooms** May to August. **Occurs** throughout much of Utah to Colorado, Nevada, Arizona, and New Mexico. Found in mixed desert scrub, desert grasslands, and sagebrush, and pinyon juniper woodlands. (5,200 to 7,800 ft)

COMMENTS: This Colorado Plateau endemic is common in the central portion of Capitol Reef. American Indians used this plant for many ceremonial and medicinal uses. The leaf fibers were used for making baskets, mats, and sandals. Another common name for Yucca is "soapweed" because it was used to make soap for cleansing. This species is similar to and may hybridize with another Yucca (*Yucca angustissima,* seen in photo inset above) found throughout Southern Utah parks and monuments.

WESTERN YARROW

Achillea millefolium | **Sunflower Family** Asteraceae

An herbaceous perennial with a strong but fairly pleasant odor. Plants grow erect, 8" to 24" tall. **Stems** and leaves are covered with stiff hairs. **Leaves** are 1¼" to 6" long and ¼" to 1¼" wide, are finely dissected, alternate, and reduced in size upwards along the stem. Leaves have a fernlike appearance. **Flower heads** contain numerous tiny white (to pinkish) flowers in broad flat topped or rounded clusters, 3" to 5" across. Tiny **seeds** are smooth. **Blooms** May to September. **Occurs** throughout Utah and North America. It grows in many soil types in desert scrub, sagebrush, pinyon juniper, ponderosa pine, Douglas fir, and spruce fir woodlands. (3,700 to 12,300 ft)

COMMENTS: It is occasionally found in Capitol Reef, Bryce Canyon, Cedar Breaks, Bears Ears, and Zion. This species has been widely used by many American Indian tribes to heal wounds. The genus name, *Achillea,* refers to the Greek hero, Achilles, who reportedly used this plant to heal soldier's wounds. The specific name, *millefolium,* means "thousand" leaves, referring to the finely dissected leaves. A European variety has been introduced for cultivation and there are differing opinions as to whether this introduced variety is spreading into the wild.

Synonyms: Achillea alpicola, Achillea angustissima, Achillea arenicola, Achillea aspleniifolia, Achillea borealis, Achillea californica, Achillea eradiata, Achillea fusca. Achillea gigantea, Achillea gracilis, Achillea lanulosa, Achillea laxiflora, Achillea megacephala, Achillea nigrescens, Achillea occidentalis, Achillea pacifica, Achillea palmeri, Achillea puberula, Achillea rosea, Achillea subalpina, Achillea tomentosa

COMMON PUSSY TOES

Antennaria parvifolia | **Sunflower Family** Asteraceae

A low growing cushion, mat forming plant only 5" to 6" tall. This species has long, horizontal stems that creep along the ground starting new plants at joints, forming the mat like growth. **Stems** and leaves are covered with woolly hairs. **Leaves** are ¼" to 1⅓" long and ⅛" to ¼" wide. Basal leaves are spatula shaped and leaves along the stem tend to be oblong to linear in shape. There are two to six flower heads per stem. These heads are about ⅓" tall and consist of numerous individual flowers with woolly **bracts**. They have the appearance of a tiny kitten's paws, hence the common name. **Flowers** tend to be white, to pink to greenish in color. **Seeds** are inconspicuous. **Blooms** May to August. **Occurs** throughout Utah, to Canada, and south to Arizona and New Mexico. It grows on uplands in sagebrush, pinyon juniper, and ponderosa pine to spruce fir communities. (5,400 to 10,600 ft)

COMMENTS: It is found in the northernmost, higher elevations of Capitol Reef, and in Bryce Canyon, Cedar Breaks and Zion. The genus name, *Antennaria,* comes from the word "antennae," as in an insect's antennae.

Synonyms: Antennaria aprica, Antennaria aureola, Antennaria holmii, Antennaria latisquamea, Antennaria minuscula, Antennaria obtusata, Antennaria pumila, Antennaria recurva, Antennaria rhodanthus

STEVIA DUSTY MAIDEN

Chaenactis stevioides | **Sunflower Family** Asteraceae

An erect annual that grows to 14" tall. Foliage is covered with fine hairs. **Leaves** are grayish green, up to 4" long, deeply lobed; fernlike and covered with soft woolly hairs. **Flowers** grow in a terminal flower head about 1" wide. White flowers are very tiny and form a small globe atop the stalk. Tiny **seeds** are hairy. **Blooms** mid April to July. **Occurs** throughout much of Utah to Nevada, California, and Wyoming. Found in dry, sandy soils on hills and benches in mixed desert scrub, sagebrush, creosote bush scrub, and pinyon juniper woodlands. (3,000 to 6,200 ft)

COMMENTS: Most commonly seen in the southern portion of Capitol Reef on the hike to Hall's Creek Narrows. This species also occurs in Arches, Canyonlands, Bears Ears, Zion, and Glen Canyon. The genus name, *Chaenactis*, comes from the Greek word *chaino*, meaning to "gape," and *actis*, meaning "ray," referring to the larger ray-like disk flowers on the outer edge of each flower head.

Synonyms: Chaenactis brachypappa, Chaenactis gillespiei, Chaenactis latifolia, Chaenactis mexicana

ROSE HEATH

Chaetopappa ericoides | **Sunflower Family** Asteraceae

A low growing, herbaceous perennial only 5" to 6" tall. It tends to grow as a small clump with many small, branching stems. **Stems** and leaves are covered with short, stiff hairs and tiny glands, such that it feels slightly sticky when touched. **Leaves** are about ⅜" long, very narrow, and linear. **Flower heads** are solitary. Only 12 to 25 ray flowers per head, they are white to pink, about ¼" long, so the entire head is about ¾" across. When plant is in full bloom, it is a small cluster of white flowers close to the ground. **Seeds** are inconspicuous. **Blooms** May to July. **Occurs** in central and southern Utah, Nevada, California, Arizona, east to Kansas and south to Mexico. It grows on uplands, hills, and mesas in mixed desert scrub to pinyon juniper communities. (5,000 to 6,000 ft)

COMMENTS: Common in the central and southern portions of Capitol Reef, and in Arches, Bryce Canyon, Canyonlands, Bears Ears, Zion, and Glen Canyon. This is a common showy daisy throughout its range.

Synonyms: Aster arenosus, Aster bellus, Aster ericaefolius, Aster hirtifolius, Aster leucelene, Inula ericoides, Leucelene ericoides, Leucelene hirtella

MAGUIRE'S DAISY

Erigeron maguirei | **Sunflower Family** Asteraceae

An herbaceous perennial reaching 11" in length, with sprawling to slightly erect stems. Base of plant is covered with old, brown leaf bases from previous year's growth. **Stems** and leaves are covered with stiff, coarse, white hairs. Basal **leaves** are ¾" to 2" long and ⅛" to ⅓" wide, spatula shaped with a rounded tip. Leaves on the stem are shorter and slightly narrower, becoming smaller near the tip. **Flower heads** are solitary to two or five per stalk; flowers white with 12 to 20 rays, about 1" wide. **Seeds** are attached to tiny, white, fluffy hairs. **Blooms** early June to late July. **Occurs** only in south central Utah. Found in pinyon juniper, ponderosa pine, and desert scrub communities. (5,400 to 7,100 ft)

COMMENTS: This Colorado Plateau endemic is a federally listed threatened species fully protected by the law.

BASIN DAISY

Erigeron pulcherrimus | **Sunflower Family** Asteraceae

An herbaceous perennial, 4" to 12" tall, with lower branches covered with shaggy bark. **Stems** and leaves are covered with stiff, gray to whitish hairs. It has very narrow basal leaves up to 2½" long. **Leaves** are entire with the upper ones becoming smaller and smaller. **Flower heads** are solitary. Ray flowers are white to pink or violet, about 1" across. **Seeds** are inconspicuous. **Blooms** May to June. **Occurs** in central and southern Utah, Colorado, Wyoming, and New Mexico. It typically grows in clay soils in desert scrub and pinyon juniper communities. (5,000 to 8,000 ft)

COMMENTS: Occasionally seen in the central portion of Capitol Reef and in Arches National Park. This species closely resembles Mound Daisy and can easily be confused with it. One way to differentiate them is that Basin Daisy has tiny leaves on the stems and Mound Daisy does not.

Synonyms: Erigeron wyomingia

SHAGGY FLEABANE

Erigeron pumilus | **Sunflower Family** Asteraceae

An herbaceous perennial that grows to 20" tall with the lower portion of the plant often covered with dried, brown leaves from previous year's growth. Leaves and **stems** are covered with spreading, coarse hairs. Plant primarily has basal leaves ¼" to 3½" long and linear. **Leaves** are entire with the upper ones becoming smaller and smaller. **Flower heads** may be numerous but occur solitary on individual stalks. Ray flowers are very numerous, white to pink, and about ½" across. Disk flowers are bright yellow. **Seeds** are inconspicuous. **Blooms** mid April to August. **Occurs** throughout Utah, Colorado, Wyoming, Idaho, California, Arizona, and New Mexico. Found in desert scrub, saltbush scrub, pinyon juniper, and ponderosa pine communities. (2,700 to 9,700 ft)

COMMENTS: Widespread throughout Capitol Reef, Arches, Bryce Canyon, Canyonlands, Bears Ears, Zion,and Glen Canyon.

CARVESEED

Glyptopleura marginata | **Sunflower Family** Asteraceae

An annual that has a very short **stem** such that it appears to sit directly on the ground. Gray-green **leaves** form a basal rosette. They are deeply dentate with prickly tips and have a milky sap when torn (3" long and ¾" wide). White **flowers** (1" to 1¼" across) grow on individual short stalks. Before flowers open, they may appear pink and as they age, they tend towards faded pink or purple in color. **Seeds** are inconspicuous. **Blooms** April to May. **Occurs** in Oregon, Idaho, California, Nevada, and Utah in desert scrub and sagebrush communities. (4,670 to 6,050 ft)

COMMENTS: This species occurs primarily in the Great Basin desert; however a few scattered populations occur in southern Utah. It is found in the very southern portions of Capitol Reef and in Glen Canyon.

ANNUAL TOWNSENDIA

Townsendia annua | **Sunflower Family** Asteraceae

An annual with primarily prostrate branches forming a low, sprawling clump. Plant can be 1" to 6" tall, but typically is only 2" to 3" tall. **Stems** and leaves are covered with stiff hairs giving them a gray green color. **Leaves** grow primarily along the stems, not basally and are ¼" to 1" long an 1/16" to ⅛" wide. They are spatula shaped to linear and entire. White or pinkish **flower heads** are ½" to 1" across. They grow on short stalks above the rest of the plant. Tiny **seeds** are covered with white fluffy hairs that resemble a small dandelion seed ball. **Blooms** mid-April to June. **Occurs** in southern Utah south to New Mexico, Arizona, Texas, and east to Colorado. Found in dry, sandy or clay soils on hills and benches in desert scrub, saltbush, and greasewood communities. (3,600 to 6,200 ft)

COMMENTS: Usually seen in the northern and central portions of Capitol Reef, and in Arches, Canyonlands, and Glen Canyon.

SILVERY TOWNSENDIA

Townsendia incana | **Sunflower Family** Asteraceae

An herbaceous perennial that forms a low growing mound. Plants tend to be 1" to 2" high and often spread out 8" to 10" forming a rounded clump. They have a well-developed root system. **Stems** are completely covered with long white hairs. **Leaves** are ⅛" to 1½" long and about 1/16" wide, spatula to lance shaped and entire. Foliage is grayish green in appearance. **Ray flowers** are white on the upper surface and pinkish on the under surface and are about ½" to ¾" across. Few to several flowers bloom at the same time and are nestled down amongst the leaves and branches. Tiny **seeds** covered with white fluffy hairs resemble a small dandelion seed ball. **Blooms** April to July. **Occurs** throughout Utah to Wyoming, New Mexico, Arizona, and Nevada. Found in dry, sandy or clay soils on hills and benches in desert scrub, saltbush, sagebrush, and pinyon juniper woodland communities. (4,300 to 9,200 ft)

COMMENTS: Found commonly throughout Capitol Reef. This is a more compact plant than the closely related annual, *T. annua*. It is the common *Townsendia* you'll see in Capitol Reef. This species is also found in Arches, Bryce Canyon, Canyonlands, Bears Ears, Zion, and Glen Canyon.

Synonyms: Townsendia arizonica, Townsendia fremontii

MOJAVE WOODY-ASTER

Xylorhiza tortifolia | **Sunflower Family** Asteraceae

A small, perennial sub-shrub that reaches to 20" tall. **Stems** are covered with long, woolly hairs. Some plants have tiny glands on the stems, also. **Leaves** are up to 4" long and ¾" wide, lance shaped to elliptical, covered with woolly hairs and have spiny dentate margins. White to bluish **flower heads** are from 1" to 3" across, with 17 to 60 ray flowers surrounding bright yellow disk flowers. **Seeds** are inconspicuous. **Blooms** April to May. **Occurs** in southern Utah, Arizona, Nevada, and California. Found in mixed desert scrub, sagebrush, blackbrush, and pinyon juniper communities. (4,000 to 7,500 ft)

COMMENTS: Found only in the southern portions of Capitol Reef. It also occurs in Glen Canyon National Recreation Area.

CISCO WOODY-ASTER

Xylorhiza venusta | **Sunflower Family** Asteraceae

A small, herbaceous perennial sub-shrub that reaches to 20" tall. **Stems** may be smooth or covered with long, straight hairs. **Leaves** occur primarily below the middle of the stem height; they are ¾" to 3½" long and up to ⅔" wide, spatula or lance shaped with the narrow end of the leaf being at the stem. White to bluish **flower heads** grow at the end of stalks. These flower stalks are up to 8" long. Flower heads are vary from ½" to 1" across, with 12 to 36 ray flowers surrounding bright yellow disk flowers. **Seeds** are inconspicuous. **Blooms** late April to June. **Occurs** in central and southern Utah and Colorado. Found in salt desert scrub communities, primarily on saline, clay soils in the Mancos and Morrison formations. (4,000 to 7,500 ft)

COMMENTS: This Colorado Plateau endemic is found in the southern portions of Capitol Reef, and in Arches, Canyonlands, and Bears Ears.

Synonyms: Aster venustus, Machaeranthera venusta

YELLOW EYE CATSPAW

Cryptantha flavoculata | **Borage Family** Boraginaceae

An herbaceous perennial that reaches 15" in height, and grows in dense tufts. One to many erect **stems** and leaves are covered with short, stiff hairs. Narrow **leaves** are entire, linear, 1¼" to 4¼" long, and 1/16" to ⅜" wide, slightly larger than the similar species, *C. flava*. The lower side of each leaf is covered with bristly hairs that have blisters or pustules at the base of each hair. White **flowers** grow in an open flower cluster 2" to 10" long. The white corolla tube is about ⅜" long, with no crests at the base. Fornices are bright yellow. **Nutlets** are lance shaped with tiny ridges running along the surface. **Blooms** mid April to July. **Occurs** throughout most of Utah, Colorado, and Wyoming to New Mexico. Associated with saltbush scrub, mixed desert scrub, pinyon juniper woodland, and ponderosa pine communities, typically on hillsides and uplands. (5,400 to 10,300 ft)

COMMENTS: Common throughout Capitol Reef, Canyonlands, Bears Ears, Zion and Glen Canyon.

Synonyms: Oreocarya flavoculata

JOHNSTON'S CRYPTANTH

Oreocarya johnstonii | **Borage Family** Boraginaceae

An herbaceous perennial that reaches 4" to 10" in height and grows from a dense basal tuft. **Stems** are 2" to 5" tall and hairy. **Leaves** are 1" to 2½" long and ¼" to 1/3" wide, covered with stiff hairs. There are small blisters or pustules at the base of each hair. This is one of the key characteristics for identifying this *Oerocarya* species. Leaves are lance shaped with the narrow end closest to the stem. Flowering stalks are conspicuous with long, spreading hairs, somewhat open and 2" to 8" long. **Flowers** are fairly large and showy, white with yellow fornices. The corolla tube is slender with abruptly flattened petal lobes that definitely surpass the calyx. The flattened lobes of the corolla are about ½" broad. **Nutlets** are smooth, shiny, and ovate in shape. **Blooms** May to June. **Occurs** only in south central Utah. Found in salt desert scrub or pinyon juniper woodlands. (4,900 to 6,400 ft)

COMMENTS: This Colorado Plateau endemic is found primarily north of Capitol Reef; however, several populations have been found in the northern portion of this park on gypsum soils with well developed biological crusts.

Synonyms: Cryptantha johnstonii

SPECTACLE POD

Dimorphocarpa wislizenii | **Mustard Family** Brassicaceae

An erect annual that reaches 20" tall. **Stems** and leaves are covered with fine, star shaped hairs. Stems may be branched or simple. Basal **leaves** are gray green, toothed to wavy margined, about 1" to 3" long and often withered and dry by the time the plant reaches full bloom. Leaves on the stems are similar in color and shape, but smaller in size. White **flowers** grow in compact clusters at the end of flowering stalks. They are ⅜" to ¾" wide. **Seedpods** are rounded and spectacle shaped, hence the common name. **Blooms** April and May. **Occurs** in south central Utah, Nevada, Colorado, Arizona, New Mexico, and south into Mexico. Found in sandy soils and sand dunes in mixed desert scrubs and desert grasslands. (2,700 to 6,900 ft)

COMMENTS: The genus, *Dimorphocarpa,* means "two types of fruit" in Latin, describing the seedpods. This species is found in the southern portions of Capitol Reef, and in Arches, Canyonlands, and Zion.

Synonyms: Dithyrea griffithsii, Dithyrea wislizenii, Dithyrea wislizeni var. griffithsii

MOUNTAIN PEPPERPLANT

Lepidium montanum | **Mustard Family** Brassicaceae

An herbaceous perennial that grows from a branched, woody rootstalk. Plants are 3" to 40" tall and bushy. **Stems** are intricately branched and often covered with fine hairs. **Leaves** are ⅛" to 4½" long, 1/16" to 1" wide, linear, and entire to narrowly lobed. Tiny white **flowers** grow on short stalks above the rest of the plant and usually cover the entire plant giving it the appearance of a bouquet of flowers rising out of the ground. **Seeds** are inconspicuous. **Blooms** May to September. **Occurs** in southern Utah, south to Arizona, Nevada, and Colorado. Found in dry, sandy to rocky soils on hills and benches in desert scrub, sagebrush, and pinyon juniper woodland communities. (2,800 to 7,000 ft)

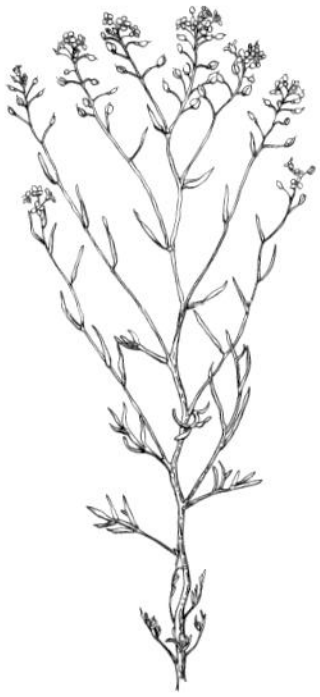

COMMENTS: Common throughout Capitol Reef, Arches, Bryce Canyon, Cedar Breaks, Bears Ears, Canyonlands, and Zion. Flowers have a fragrant, sweet smell and the seeds taste like black pepper.

Synonyms: Lepidium albiflorum, Lepidium corymbosum, Lepidium philonitrum Lepidium scopulorum f. canescens

TALL THELYPODY

Thelypodium integrifolium | **Mustard Family** Brassicaceae

A biennial that reaches 2' to 10' in height, with mostly simple, smooth stems. Basal **leaves** are spatula to lance shaped or even egg shaped with entire or toothed margins, and are 2" to 12" long and $\frac{2}{3}$" to 4" wide. Leaves on the stem are much smaller and mainly elliptical to lance shaped. **Flowers** cluster at the very tips of branches, grow on short stalks, and are white to lavender with purplish sepals. Each flower is about $\frac{1}{4}$" wide. **Seedpods** are long and thin, $\frac{3}{8}$" to $1\frac{3}{4}$" long, and curve upwards. **Blooms** July to November. **Occurs** throughout much of Utah to Nebraska, the Dakotas, Washington, Oregon, and Colorado. Found in moist sites, along streams, in seeps or springs. Tolerates alkaline soils fairly well. (3,000 to 7,000 ft)

COMMENTS: Found in riparian areas in the central and southern portions of Capitol Reef, and in Arches, Canyonlands, Bears Ears, Zion, and Glen Canyon.

Synonyms: Pachypodium integrifolium

HOOKER'S SANDWORT

Eremogone hookeri | **Pink Family** Caryophyllaceae

A perennial herb that grows as a small to moderately sized compact cushion mound. **Stems** are only about 2" long. Plants have shiny basal **leaves** up to 2" long. Leaves grow in pairs on stems and have papery thin margins. Leaves have a distinctive odor when crushed. Tiny, white **flowers** grow in congested clusters at the tip of stalks and typically cover the entire mound when plant in full bloom. Plants appear as a white ball growing on the ground. **Seeds** are inconspicuous. **Blooms** May to July. **Occurs** throughout much of Utah, to Nevada, Wyoming, Nebraska, and Colorado. Found in sandy soils in sagebrush, mixed desert scrub, and pinyon juniper woodland. (5,700 to 9,600 ft)

COMMENTS: This beautiful little cushion plant is found in the northern portions of Capitol Reef.

Synonyms: Arenaria hookeri

GREENLEAF MANZANITA

Arctostaphylos patula | **Heath Family** Ericaceae

A large, rounded shrub with stout, reddish branches up to 3' tall and often wider than tall. It often forms dense stands that are very difficult to walk through. **Branches** are intricately twisted, deep red in color and may appear to be varnished or waxed. Erect **leaves** are oval to egg shaped, ¾" to 2" in long and nearly as broad; they are yellow green to bright green and may be covered with tiny glands or simply smooth. **Flowers** grow in dense, drooping clusters; they are urn shaped, whitish to pink in color, about ⅓" in length. Fruits are small globe shaped, creamy white to brownish berries. **Blooms** May to June. **Occurs** from Oregon south to Arizona and east to Colorado. Found in ponderosa pine woodlands, in clay to sandy soils. In the southwest U.S., it is often found in sandstone canyons. (4,500 to 10,000 ft)

COMMENTS: This shrub is highly valued as forage for wildlife and birds. American Indians used the leaves for medicinal purposes and harvested the berries for eating. The bark and stems were used for making dyes. It is found throughout Capitol Reef. In the northern portions, it occurs on open slopes in ponderosa pine woodlands, and in the central and southern portions, it is restricted to canyons and shady areas. It also occurs in Bryce Canyon, Cedar Breaks, Bears Ears, Glen Canyon, and Zion.

Synonyms: Arctostaphylos acutifolia, Arctostaphylos parryana var. pinetorum, Arctostaphylos pungens var. platyphylla

MILKWEED MILKVETCH

Astragalus asclepiadoides | **Pea Family** Fabaceae

A tall, erect perennial up to 2' tall. An unusual *Astragalus* that has entire, oval leaves rather than the typical compound leaves with multiple leaflets. **Leaves** give this plant the appearance of a milkweed, hence the common name. They are round to oval, alternate, and up to 2½" broad. **Flower** stalks barely surpass the leafy branch and have two to 12 flowers per stalk. The purplish to cream colored flowers strongly curve upwards at full bloom. They are about ½" to 1" long. **Seedpods** also curve upwards, are borne on a short stalk, and are strongly inflated and oval in shape (1½" long and to ½" wide). **Blooms** April to June. **Occurs** in south central Utah and Colorado. This is a Colorado Plateau endemic found in fine textured, seleniferous clay soils in mixed desert scrub communities. (4,200 to 7,600 ft)

COMMENTS: Found uncommonly in the central and northern portions of Capitol Reef. Plant is slightly ill scented and is a selenium indicator.

GREAT RUSHY MILKVETCH

Astragalus lonchocarpus | **Pea Family** Fabaceae

A bushy perennial 12" to 33" tall. It often forms a bush as broad as it is tall. Compound **leaves** are ¾" to 5" long, with three to nine leaflets that are ¾" to 1½" long and less than ¼" wide. Leaflets are linear to ovate and may be rounded at the base. They may be hairy or smooth on either or both sides. **Flower** stalks are open and may be up to 9" long, each stalk has seven to 40 flowers. The whitish to cream colored flowers are spreading or dip downwards at full bloom. They are about ½" to ¾" long. Flower tube is cylindrical and woolly with hairs. **Seedpods** hang downwards, are borne on a short stalk, are elliptical to oblong in shape, and about 1" to 2" long. Pods have one chamber. **Blooms** late April to July. **Occurs** throughout Utah, to Colorado, New Mexico, Arizona, and Nevada. Found on benches and canyon bottoms in sandy soils in mixed desert scrub and pinyon juniper woodlands. (3,800 to 8,300 ft)

COMMENTS: Found in the central and northern portions of Capitol Reef, often seen blooming along Highway 24 near the Visitor Center. It also occurs in Bryce Canyon, Canyonlands, Cedar Breaks, and Glen Canyon.

STINKING MILKVETCH

Astragalus praelongus | **Pea Family** Fabaceae

A perennial herb 4" to 36" tall. It often forms a scraggly clump with erect **stems**. Foliage is covered with short stiff hairs. Compound **leaves** are 1" to 9" long, with seven to 33 leaflets up to 2" long and elliptical to egg shaped. **Flower** stalks are up to 10" long, each stalk has ten to 33 flowers. The whitish to cream colored flowers may be tipped with purple and hang downward at full bloom. They are about ½" to 1" long. **Seedpods** may hang down or tip upright, are inflated in an elliptical to egg shape, and are about 1" to 1½" long. Pods dry tan colored and woody. They stay on the plant through the fall and into winter. **Blooms** April to July. **Occurs** throughout Utah, Colorado, New Mexico, and Arizona. Found on benches and uplands in clay, seleniferous soils of the Mancos Shale, Moenkopi, and Chinle formations in mixed desert scrub and pinyon juniper woodlands (2,500 to 8,300 ft)

COMMENTS: Found in the central and southern portions of Capitol Reef. Most often seen by visitors around the Visitor Center and along Highway 24 through Fruita. It also occurs in Arches, Bryce Canyon, Canyonlands, Glen Canyon, and Zion. This species has a strong unpleasant odor, hence the common name.

CANYONLANDS PRAIRIE CLOVER

Dalea flavescens | **Pea Family** Fabaceae

A large herbaceous perennial up to 20" tall, that grows as a bushy shrub. **Leaves** are up to 1¾" long, with three to seven leaflets. Leaflets are about 5/8" long and up to ⅜" wide, linear to oblong, or elliptic. Each leaflet has fine hairs on both surfaces, and glands on the undersurface. The terminal leaflet is continuous on the rachis. Floral spikes are typically open and spreading, ½" to 3½" long; bracts are ⅛" to ¼" long, and covered with long, soft, shaggy hairs. **Flowers** are white, fading to cream color; the style is nearly ⅜" long. **Seedpods** have long, woolly hairs covering them. **Blooms** May to July. **Occurs** in south central Utah and Arizona. Found in mixed desert scrub, and blackbrush communities, usually in wash bottoms with sandy soils. (4,700 to 5,000 ft)

COMMENTS: Species characteristics may vary throughout its range, making this a difficult species to identify. It is typically seen in the southern portion of Capitol Reef, and in Arches, Canyonlands, Bears Ears, and Glen Canyon.

Synonyms: Dalea epica, Dalea flavescens var. epica, Petalostemon flavescens

WILD LICORICE

Glycyrrhiza lepidota | **Pea Family** Fabaceae

An erect, perennial herb that reaches 4' tall. Compound **leaves** are 3" to 7½" long, with 13 to 19 leaflets that are ⅓" to 2" long and up to ⅔" wide. Leaves are oblong to lance shaped with pointed tips and are dotted with tiny glands and hairs on the underside. White to cream **flowers** grow on elongated stalks containing 20 to 50 flowers each. Flowers are about ½" long, erect when in full bloom, and have a bell shaped calyx. **Seedpods** spread outwards, are oblong, laterally compressed, about ¾" long, and covered with hooked prickles. **Blooms** mid April to June. **Occurs** throughout most of the United States, except in the southeast. Found in moist areas such as along streams and springs. (2,200 to 8,100 ft)

COMMENTS: Found in riparian areas in the central portion of Capitol Reef, and in Arches, Canyonlands, Glen Canyon, and Zion. American Indians have used this species for centuries to treat bronchial illnesses, stomach problems, and even as a mouth wash to keep breath fresh and clean. The genus name, *Glycyrrhiza,* comes from the Latin terms *glykos*, meaning "sweet" and *rhiza*, meaning "root," referring to the sweet roots. Reportedly, the roots were cooked and eaten by American Indians and early pioneers.

Synonyms: Glycyrrhiza glutinosa, Glycyrrhiza lepidota var. glutinosa

SMALL LEAF GERANIUM

Geranium caespitosum | **Geranium Family** Geraniaceae

An herbaceous perennial reaching 6" to 25" tall with a woody base. **Stems** are sprawling to erect and covered with angled hairs and glands. **Leaves** grow on a short stalk, are palmately lobed, and each of five lobes usually have three teeth; they are typically 1½" wide and up to 2¾" long. **Flowers** grow singly or in pairs on a short stalk and are white or pink to lavender, often with purple veins running lengthwise on the petal. Flowers are about 1" across. **Seedpods** are shaped like a crane's bill (*Geranium* means "crane flower") that splits longitudinally to scatter seeds widely. **Blooms** June to August. **Occurs** in south central Utah, Colorado, New Mexico, and Arizona. Found in sagebrush, pinyon juniper, ponderosa pine, and aspen woodlands. (6,000 to 11,000 ft)

COMMENTS: Found along Pleasant Creek and in the northern portions of Capitol Reef. It also occurs in Bryce Canyon, Cedar Breaks, Bears Ears, and Zion. American Indians use plants in this genus for numerous medicinal purposes. Many wild geranium species are high in tannins and were used by American Indians for tanning of hides.

Synonyms: Geranium thermale

FENDLERBUSH

Fendlera rupicola | **Hydrangea Family** Hydrangeaceae

A large, erect shrub with stiff, intricate branches; plants reach 3' to 6' in height. Bark on **stems** is grooved lengthwise, and typically reddish or tan colored. **Leaves** are opposite, linear to elliptical or occasionally oval, ⅜" to 1⅛" long, and slightly hairy on both sides. The mid rib of each leaf is prominent. Large white **flowers** are solitary on the end of short branches. The four petals are very showy and distinctive in shape; flowers reach about 1½" across. **Seed** capsules are small. **Blooms** late April to June. **Occurs** in southern Utah, Colorado, Arizona, and Texas. Found in rocky, sandstone cracks and ledges in blackbrush, mixed desert scrub, and pinyon juniper woodlands. (4,200 to 7,900 ft)

COMMENTS: May be found in the southern portion of Capitol Reef, Arches, Canyonlands, and Glen Canyon. Plants are commonly found southeast of Hanksville, Utah. The genus was named for Augustus Fendler, an early botanist and explorer of the southwest. American Indians used the wood from this plant to make arrows and digging sticks since it is a hard, dense wood.

Synonyms: Fendlera rupicola var. falcata

SEGO LILY

Calochortus nuttallii | **Lily Family** Liliaceae

An erect lily, up to 20" tall, although typically much shorter, with a main stalk and usually three leaves. It grows from a bulb buried in the ground. Simple, linear **leaves** may lie on the ground slightly curled or be erect. Tulip shaped **flowers** are 1" to 1½" across, may be white, cream or lavender in color. The sepals are purplish to greenish in color. A large, hair covered gland is located in a patch of yellow at the inner base of each petal. These glands are occasionally bordered by a magenta crescent. **Seeds** are three angled capsules 1" to 2" long. **Blooms** May to July. **Occurs** throughout Utah and from the Midwestern States to Nevada, Arizona, and New Mexico. Typically grows in sandy soils in saltbush, greasewood, grasslands, and ponderosa pine woodlands. (3,300 to 10,000 feet)

COMMENTS: This is the Utah state wildflower. American Indians and pioneers ate the bulbs, which are said to taste like potatoes. However, attempts to cultivate this lily have been unsuccessful so plants should never be harvested from the wild or soon we would not have this beautiful wildflower to enjoy. It is occasionally found throughout Capitol Reef. After wet winters, large fields of these lilies can be seen along the Notom Road in the Strike Valley. It can also be found in all the Southern Utah land units. A yellow species or variety of this species (*Calochortus aureus* or *C. n. var. aureus*, depending on the botanical source) also occurs in Capitol Reef. *Calochortus* comes from two Greek words meaning "beautiful grass."

SWEET SAND VERBENA

Abronia fragrans | **Four O'clock Family** Nyctaginaceae

A low, spreading perennial herb that typically grows 7" to 10" tall. Opposite **leaves** are on a short stalk; they are egg shaped, fleshy and ⅜" to 3½" long. Foliage may be smooth or more typically covered with sticky glandular hairs that attract sand grains. Trumpet shaped **flowers** grow in dense terminal clusters. They are white to pinkish, fragrant and ⅜" to 1" long. Petals are lobed and flared at the end. The end of the stalk that bears the flower parts is rounded or cone shaped. (In contrast to Sandpuffs, *Tripterocalyx micranthus*, where the stalk end is flat in shape.) **Seeds** may or may not be winged, if so, wings are thick and not continuous around the entire fruit. **Blooms** May to August. **Occurs** throughout Utah to Montana, Nevada, Arizona, New Mexico, and Texas and south to Mexico. Found in sandy soils in mixed desert scrub, sagebrush, pinyon juniper, and ponderosa pine woodlands. (2,500 to 8,200 ft)

COMMENTS: This species is widespread and common throughout Capitol Reef, and in Arches, Bryce Canyon, Canyonlands, Glen Canyon, and Zion. American Indians used this species to treat stomach and bowel problems.

Synonyms: Abronia nudata, Abronia texana

NARROWLEAF UMBRELLAWORT

Mirabilis linearis | **Four O'Clock Family** Nyctaginaceae

A tall herbaceous perennial that grows up to 40" tall. **Leaves** are sessile or may be on a short stalk; they are linear ¾" to 4" long, and some may be toothed. **Flowers** grow in a terminal clusters, usually in a group of three. They are white to pinkish, ½" wide with a short, flaring tube. Petals are deeply lobed. **Seeds** are inconspicuous. **Blooms** July to August. **Occurs** throughout Utah and the western States. Found in mixed desert scrub, sagebrush, rabbitbrush, pinyon juniper, ponderosa pine, riparian areas, and spruce fir communities. (3,700 to 10,000 ft)

COMMENTS: It is widespread and common throughout Capitol Reef and all the Southern Utah land units. American Indians in the Great Plains region used this species in a tea to treat urinary tract problems. This specific name, *linearis*, refers to the linear leaves.

Synonyms: Allionia decumbens, Allionia gausapoides, Allionia linearius, Calymenia decumbens, Mirabilis decumbens, Mirabilis diffusa, Mirabilis gausapoides, Mirabilis hirsusta var. linearis, Mirabilis lanceolata, Oxybaphus angustifolius, Oxybaphus decumbens, Oxybaphus diffusus, Oxybaphus gausapoides, Oxybaphus lanceolatus, Oxybaphus linearis, Oxybaphus linearis var. subhispidus

WHITESTEM EVENING PRIMROSE

Oenothera albicaulis | **Evening Primrose Family** Onagraceae

An annual herb that grows to 10" tall, with erect, whitish stems. Basal **leaves** are ⅜" to 4" long, grow in a rosette, and are generally entire, while stem leaves are deeply lobed. This difference in basal and stem leaf shapes is a good way to distinguish this species from Pale evening primrose. Large, white **flowers** are nodding in bud, and turn pinkish with age. **Seed** capsules are erect, ¾" to 1½" long. **Blooms** mid March to August. **Occurs** in southeastern Utah, Arizona, Texas, Mexico, Montana, Colorado, and South Dakota. Found in sandy soils of bottomlands, hills, uplands, or mesas in desert scrub, grasslands, and pinyon juniper woodlands. Found along roadsides or other sandy disturbed places. (4,100 to 6,000 ft)

COMMENTS: It occurs in the central and southern portions of Capitol Reef, most commonly seen on the hike to Hall's Creek Narrows. It also occurs in Bryce Canyon, Canyonlands, Bears Ears, Glen Canyon, and Zion. Navajo Indians have several medicinal uses for this species, including treating boils, spider bites, kidney disease, and other sores. They also use it in ceremonies.

Synonyms: Anogra albicaulis, Oenothera ctenophylla

TUFTED OR FRAGRANT EVENING PRIMROSE

Oenothera caespitosa | **Evening Primrose Family** Onagraceae

A stemless, perennial herb growing from a basal rosette of leaves. **Leaves** are up to 10" long and up to 1" wide with entire, lobed, or toothed margins and covered with soft hairs. White **flowers** are 2½" to 3¼" in diameter, are quite fragrant, and turn pinkish or purplish with age. Flowers may be sessile in the rosette of leaves, or solitary on a stalk. **Seed** capsules are erect, rather small (⅛"), and hard. **Blooms** mid-April to September. **Occurs** throughout Utah, from Canada to Nevada, east to Colorado and Nebraska. It prefers sandy soils in sandy or rocky areas of hills, washes, or uplands, in desert scrub, pinyon juniper, and mixed conifer woodlands. (4,000 to 8,500 ft)

COMMENTS: It is showy when blooming and can easily be seen along roadsides throughout Capitol Reef and all the Southern Utah land units. Buds open in the evening to be pollinated by moths. Pliny the Elder, a Roman writer and encyclopedic who was the foremost authority on science in the first century AD, used the name *Oenothera* for a plant (now unknown) that was reputed to cause sleep when its juices were drunk with wine. The word itself comes from the Greek word *oinotheras*, which has several derivations: "wine scenting," since its roots were used for this purpose; "wine imbibing," from *oinos* for "wine" and *thera* for "imbibing"; or "donkey chase," from *onos* for "donkey" and *thera* for "chase or hunting." *Synonyms: Pachylophus caespitosa*

PALE EVENING PRIMROSE

Oenothera pallida | **Evening Primrose Family** Onagraceae

An erect perennial herb that can reach 28" in height, but is more typically seen about 12" high. These plants usually have a straggly, somewhat sprawling appearance. The surface of the white **stems** is often flaky. **Leaves** are very narrow; often linear shaped, with entire, toothed, or lobed margins ⅜" to 3⅛" long and ⅛" to ¾" wide). Leaves growing at the base of plant and along the stem are similar in shape, in contrast to those of whitestem evening primrose. Pale white **flowers**, up to 4" across, fade to pink or cream as they age. **Seed** capsules are up to 2" long and very narrow; may be curved or straight. **Blooms** May to September. **Occurs** throughout Utah into Arizona, New Mexico, Texas, Nevada, eastern Washington, Colorado, and Wyoming. Found in gravely to sandy soils of uplands, hills, or canyons in sagebrush, desert scrub, pinyon juniper woodland, and ponderosa pine communities. (6,500 to 8,300 ft)

COMMENTS: Fairly common and widespread throughout Capitol Reef, and Arches, Bryce Canyon, Canyonlands, Bears Ears, Glen Canyon, and Zion.

UTE'S LADIES TRESSES

Spiranthes diluvialis | **Orchid Family** Orchidaceae

An erect, slender plant ranging from 3" to 24" tall. Two to four basal **leaves** are 1" to 12" long, ⅛" to ½" wide and linear to lance shaped. There are two to six leaves on the stem that are greatly reduced in size. **Floral bracts** are oval to lance shaped, flowers creamy white, ⅓" to ½" long. **Seeds** are inconspicuous. **Blooms** June to September (depending on elevation). **Occurs** in several counties in Utah, Nevada, and Colorado. **Found** along streams, rivers, in bogs, and open seep areas in cottonwood, tamarisk, and willow thickets. (4,400 to 7,000 ft)

COMMENTS: This is a federally listed threatened species that historically occurred along the Fremont River in Capitol Reef and was last seen in the Park in the late 1990s. National Park Service personnel continue to survey for this species in Capitol Reef. It is difficult to distinguish this rare species from the more common *Spiranthes romanzoffiana*, however, *S. diluvialis* is typically found at much lower elevations.

ARMED PRICKLY POPPY

Argemone munita | **Poppy Family** Papaveraceae

An upright perennial herb that closely resembles a thistle; plants range from 1' to 3' in height and are covered with stout spines. **Stems** and leaves may be coated with a waxy covering giving the plant a gray green appearance. **Leaves** reach up to 6" long, are lance to oval in shape, and are armed with stout spines on toothed edges and along the veins. White **flowers** are large and showy with crinkly petals; flowers are 3" to 5" across. **Seed** capsules are spiny, shaped similar to a football, and can reach up to 2" in length. **Blooms** June to August. **Occurs** in southern Utah, California, Nevada, and New Mexico south to Mexico. Found in mixed desert scrub communities often in sandy soils and disturbed sites as such along roadsides. (2,500 to 7,500 ft)

COMMENTS: This genus has numerous medicinal properties and has been used by American Indians for centuries. It is found in the southern portion of Capitol Reef, and in Glen Canyon and Zion.

PALMER'S PENSTEMON

Penstemon palmeri Plantago | **Figwort Family** Plantaginaceae

A sturdy, perennial herb 24" to 50" tall with few to many erect stems. Foliage and **stems** are gray green in color. Second and third year plants may appear as a bushy shrub. **Leaves** are ¾" to 4 ½" long, entire, elliptical, with wavy, toothed margins. Lower leaves grow on a short stalk, while upper ones are clasping and smaller in size. Pink to cream, inflated, tubular **flowers** grow in an elongated spike. Each flower has magenta colored stripes running lengthwise in the inflated tube. Flowers are up to 1½" long. They extend outward when in full bloom. **Seeds** are inconspicuous. **Blooms** mid May to July. **Occurs** primarily in central and southern Utah, Nevada, California, and Arizona. Found in sandy soils on canyon bottoms or benches in mixed desert scrub, pinyon juniper woodlands, and ponderosa pine communities. (2,600 to 9,000 ft)

COMMENTS: Found throughout Capitol Reef, common in Grand Wash, Capitol Gorge, and the Burr Trail switchbacks. It also occurs in Bears Ears, Canyonlands, Glen Canyon, and Zion.

ROSY SKYROCKET

Ipomopsis roseata | **Phlox Family** Polemoniaceae

A small, perennial sub-shrub that is slightly woody above the rootstalk, with stems reaching 14" tall. **Stems** are may be covered with short hairs and occasionally tiny glands that attract grains of sand when the wind blows. **Leaves** are mainly on the stems, linear, typically lobed and approximately 1½" long. Tiny white **flowers** grow in compact, terminal round-topped clusters. **Seeds** are inconspicuous. **Blooms** May to July. **Occurs** in south central Utah and Colorado. Found in blackbrush, mixed desert scrub, pinyon juniper woodland, and sagebrush communities. (3,900 to 7,500 ft)

COMMENTS: This is a Colorado Plateau endemic species. It is found in the central portion of Capitol Reef, and in Arches, Canyonlands, Bears Ears, and Glen Canyon. It is such a nondescript plant that it is rarely noticed unless in full bloom.

Synonyms: Gilia roseata

PRICKLY PHLOX

Linanthus pungens | **Phlox Family** Polemoniaceae

A perennial sub-shrub that grows 4" to 16" tall. Most of the branching occurs below the center of the plant. **Stems** are covered with small prickly leaves. Narrow green **leaves** (about ½" long) may be palmately or pinnately lobed and are always spine tipped. White to cream colored **flowers** have five petals and a long narrow tube. They grow from the tip of each stem. Flowers open at night and close during the day, so in early morning you will see a beautiful white bouquet of flowers covering the plant. They are pollinated by moths at night. **Seeds** are inconspicuous. **Blooms** May to September. **Occurs** in the western U.S., north to Canada and south to Mexico. Found in sandy to rocky soils in sagebrush, pinyon-juniper, to ponderosa pine forests. (5,600 to 7,000 ft)

COMMENTS: It is common in Capitol Reef where it occurs in sandy soils from Pleasant Creek south to Halls Creek. It also occurs in Arches, Bryce Canyon, Canyonlands, Glen Canyon, Bears Ears, and Zion. Navajos use this species for medicinal purposes.

Synonyms: Leptodactylon pungens, Gilia hallii, Gilia hookeri, Gilia pungens, Leptodactylon hazeliae, Leptodactylon lilacinum

DESERT PHLOX

Phlox austromontana | **Phlox Family** Polemoniaceae

An herbaceous perennial that grows as a low mat forming plant, usually 3" to 12" wide and only a couple inches tall. **Stems** are covered with long, soft hairs. **Leaves** are opposite, linear and about ¾" long. The blue, white or lavender **flowers** are nestled into the branch tips, about ⅜" across, bell shaped with five flaring lobes. **Seeds** are inconspicuous. **Blooms** April to June. **Occurs** throughout much of Utah, Arizona, California, and Nevada. Found in sagebrush, mixed desert scrub, saltbush scrub, pinyon juniper woodland, and ponderosa pine communities. (4,000 to 10,000 ft)

COMMENTS: This showy wildflower can be seen throughout Capitol Reef on upland benches and slopes. It also occurs in Arches, Bryce Canyon, Zion, and Glen Canyon. The Greek word *Phlox* means "flame," referring to the brightly colored flowers in this genus. When flowers are in bud, the petal edges are folded to overlap the next petal.

CRISP-LEAF BUCKWHEAT

Eriogonum corymbosum | **Buckwheat Family** Polygonaceae

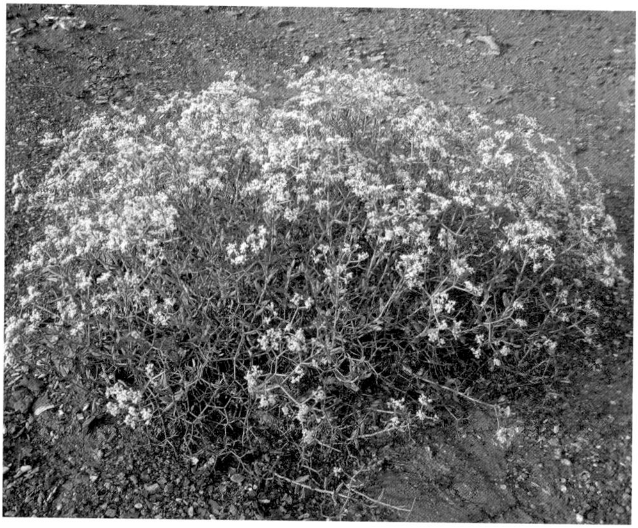

A fairly large clump forming shrub that reaches up to 4' tall and is just about as wide. In our area it is usually about 18" to 24" tall. This is a complex and highly variable species. **Leaves** are lance shaped, elliptical, oval, or rounded, ¼" to 1½" long. Leaves may be densely covered with fine woolly hairs or smooth and free of hairs on one or both sides. The tiny white or yellow **flowers** grow in flat topped, terminal clusters on naked flower stalks. Flowers lack petals but have petal like sepals. **Seeds** are inconspicuous. **Blooms** August to November. **Occurs** throughout much of Utah, to Arizona, and Colorado. Found on sandy to clay soils in mixed desert scrub, sagebrush, blackbrush, pinyon juniper woodland, and ponderosa pine communities. (3,000 to 9,000 ft)

COMMENTS: The yellow flowered phase of this species has been put into a separate variety (see *Eriogonum corymbosum var. aureum*). Some species of *Eriogonum* hybridize, which makes identification of these plants challenging. This buckwheat is common throughout Capitol Reef, particularly along the scenic drive and in Fruita. It also occurs in Arches, Bryce Canyon, Canyonlands, Bears Ears, Glen Canyon, and Zion. The specific name, *corymbosum,* refers to the flat-topped inflorescence.

Synonyms: Eriogonum effusum var. durum

BUTTERFLY BUCKWHEAT

Eriogonum leptocladon var. papiliunculi | **Buckwheat Family** Polygonaceae

A large clump forming shrub that reaches up to 30" tall. Plants have slender, intricately branching, smooth **stems**, yellow green in color. **Leaves** are linear, ⅜" to 1¾" long, found primarily at the lower portion of the stems. Plant appears to be leafless when in full bloom. The tiny whitish **flowers** grow on elongated, unbranched flower stalks. Flowers lack petals but have petal like sepals. **Seeds** are inconspicuous. **Blooms** August to November. Occurs in southern Utah and Arizona. Found on sandy soils (even in sand dunes) in sand sagebrush, blackbrush, and desert grasslands. (4,300 to 6,200 ft)

COMMENTS: This variety of *Eriogonum leptocladon* is a Colorado Plateau endemic. It is found in the southern portions of Capitol Reef and in Glen Canyon. It can also be found in the Notom area, east of Capitol Reef.

WHITE VIRGIN'S BOWER

Clematis ligusticifolia | **Buttercup Family** Ranunculaceae

A woody vine that reaches 30' or more in length covering other vegetation with sprawling **stems** and white flowers. Opposite, compound **leaves** have three to seven toothed or lobed leaflets. Leaflets are pointed at the tip and may be lance or oval in shape. **Flowers** lack petals but have showy, white to cream sepals that are ¼" to ½" long. Male and female flowers are on separate plants. **Seeds** are borne in a dense, white fuzzy cluster up to 2" in length. **Blooms** June to July. **Occurs** throughout Utah, California, Colorado, Arizona, New Mexico, north to North Dakota and Canada. It typically grows canyons and along streams in riparian communities. (4,000 to 8,000 feet)

COMMENTS: It is widespread throughout Capitol Reef. It also occurs in Arches, Bryce Canyon, Canyonlands, Bears Ears, Zion, and Glen Canyon. Both American Indians and pioneers used this plant for medicinal purposes. It is valuable forage for wildlife and cover for birds.

UTAH SERVICEBERRY

Amelanchier utahensis | **Rose Family** Rosaceae

A moderate to large erect shrub (up to 12' tall), with numerous intricate branches. Shrubs are intricately branched with reddish stems, but no thorns. **Leaves** are oval to egg shaped. Upper surface of the leaves is usually a bright green while the underside is covered with fine hairs giving it a more grayish appearance. Leaf margins are finely toothed near the tip. Showy, fragrant, white **flowers** are found in clusters at the tips of **branchlets**; petals ⅜" to ¾" long, with wide open spacing between each petal. Berries are purple to deep blue and full of tiny seeds. **Blooms** May to June. **Occurs** throughout Utah, Washington to Baja California, Arizona to Mexico, and east to Texas. Found on dry slopes or in washes and canyon bottoms in desert scrub, pinyon juniper woodland, ponderosa pine, and chaparral communities. (3,100 to 7,500 ft)

COMMENTS: It is common and widespread throughout Capitol Reef, and in all the Southern Utah land units. Berries from these plants were an important food source for American Indians. Early settlers included the berries in their pemmican and other foods.

Synonyms: Amelanchier rubescens var. cinerea

APACHE PLUME

Fallugia paradoxa | **Rose Family** Rosaceae

A large, erect shrub (up to 5' in height), with numerous intricate **branches**. The bark is streaked alternately chocolate brown and grayish white, often peeling or flaky. Alternate wedge-shaped **leaves** grow in clusters along the **branchlets**, and are primarily three lobed (may be five lobed). Upper surface of the leaves is covered with greenish scales or bumps, and the underside is covered with minute reddish to rust colored scales or bumps. (The underside leaf color is one of the features for telling Apache Plume from Cliffrose.) Showy white **flowers** are solitary at the tips of branchlets, petals are ½" to ¾" long. Pistils are numerous, and the style is plume-like. **Seeds** have a purplish cluster of feathery plumes nearly an inch long attached to them. **Blooms** mid-April to July. **Occurs** in southern Utah, Nevada, and California, south through Arizona to Mexico, and east to Texas. Found in sandy soils in washes or canyon bottoms in desert scrub and pinyon juniper woodlands. (3,100 to 7,500 ft)

COMMENTS: It is common throughout Capitol Reef, but particularly abundant in Grand Wash and Capitol Gorge. It also occurs in Bryce Canyon, Canyonlands, Glen Canyon, and Zion. Hopi Indians prepared the leaves for use as a stimulant for hair growth. Other medicinal uses include preparing the roots for use to ease joint aches or coughs. The genus, *Fallugia,* is named after Italian abbot Virgilio Fallugi, a botanical writer. *Paradoxa* comes from the "paradox" of new flowers and seeds intermingling on the shrub throughout the growing season.

Synonyms: Fallugia micrantha, Sieversia paradoxa

ROCK SPIRAEA

Petrophytum caespitosum | **Rose Family** Rosaceae

A long-lived, mat forming shrub that can cover large areas of rock. **Leaves** are spatula shaped to oblong, ⅛" to ¾" long and very narrow. They are usually covered with long, straight hairs. Tiny clusters of white **flowers** are borne on a short stalk and grow in a dense little globe. **Seeds** are inconspicuous. **Blooms** July to September. **Occurs** throughout much of Utah, Oregon to South Dakota, California, and south to Arizona, New Mexico, and Texas. Found on rock faces, in rock crevices and hanging gardens where it clings to the rock, or if the rock erodes beneath, it will hang down from its stout rootstalk. (3,500 to 10,000 ft)

COMMENTS: The genus name, *Petrophytum,* means "rock plant," referring to its habit of clinging to rock faces. It is most commonly seen in the central portion of Capitol Reef. It also occurs in Arches, Canyonlands, Bears Ears, Glen Canyon, and Zion.

Synonyms: Spiraea caespitosa var. elatior

CLIFFROSE

Purshia mexicana | **Rose Family** Rosaceae

A large, erect, evergreen shrub up to 8' tall, with numerous intricate **branches**. The bark shreds easily from the main branches, which gives the shrub a scruffy appearance. Plants are very fragrant while in bloom. **Leaves** grow in clusters along the branchlets, are wedge shaped and primarily five lobed. Upper surface of the leaves is covered with minute greenish scales or bumps, and the underside is white woolly. (The underside leaf color is one of the features for telling Cliffrose apart from Apache Plume.) Showy white, yellow, or cream-colored **flowers** have five petals; flowers are ½" to 1" across. **Seeds** have feathery plumes slightly over an inch long. **Blooms** mid April to July. **Occurs** throughout much of Utah, Nevada, California, Arizona, Colorado, New Mexico, and south to Mexico. Found on dry slopes or canyon bottoms in mixed desert scrub, pinyon juniper woodland, and ponderosa pine communities. (2,700 to 9,000 ft)

COMMENTS: It is common throughout Capitol Reef, and particularly abundant in Grand Wash and Capitol Gorge. It also occurs in all the other Southern Utah land units. American Indians used the shaggy bark to make mats and clothing and the branches for making arrows. This plant is favored forage for several species of wildlife.

Synonyms: Cowania mexicana

SACRED DATURA

Datura wrightii | **Potato Family** Solanaceae

A robust annual or perennial herb that grows to 4½' tall. **Stems** are erect, covered with short, grayish hairs. Large, dark green **leaves** are 2" to 10" long; egg shaped and may be toothed along the margins. Stems and leaves have a rather strong, unpleasant odor. Large, showy, trumpet shaped white **flowers** stand out above the rest of the plant. Flowers are up to 6" long and sweetly scented. Golf ball sized fruits are prickly. **Blooms** June to October. **Occurs** in central and southern Utah, Colorado, Texas, California, and south to Mexico. Found in creosote bush, sagebrush, mixed desert scrub, and pinyon juniper woodlands. (2,300 to 6,100 ft)

COMMENTS: All parts of this plant are toxic and highly poisonous. Even touching the leaves can leave toxic chemicals on your fingers, so be safe and don't touch! American Indians were known to use this plant to produce hallucinations during ceremonies. Because of its extreme toxicity and highly variable potency, only a few highly trained individuals were allowed to use the plant. It is found in the central and southern portions of Capitol Reef, and in Arches, Canyonlands, Bears Ears, Glen Canyon, and Zion.

Synonyms: Datura innoxia var. quinquecuspidata, Datura metel var. quinquecuspida

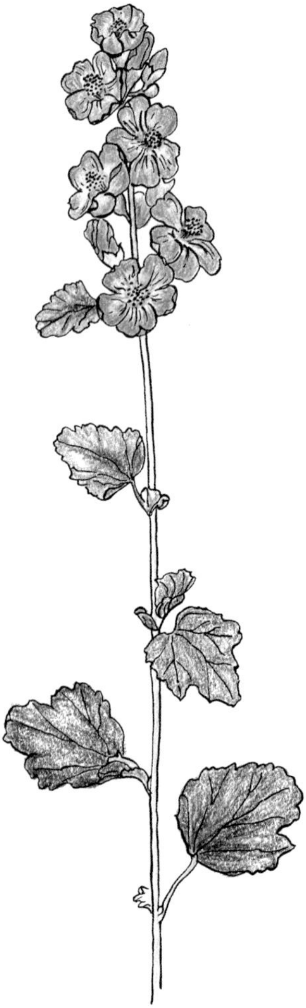

YELLOW AND ORANGE FLOWERS

SHINY LEAF SPRING PARSLEY

Aulospermum purpureum | **Carrot Family** Apiaceae

A bright, shiny green herbaceous perennial that is 2" to 10" tall. Plants tend to grow more flattened along the ground rather than erect and upright. They may have a single or multiple **stems** that grow to just above ground level. **Leaves** are primarily basal, are up to 8" long (including the leaf stalk), and are two to three times pinnately compound with up to four opposite pairs of lateral leaflets. The leaflets are oblong to ovate in shape with rounded to pointed teeth. One to five flowering stalks are up to 8" tall. Bright yellow **flowers** are borne in a flat-topped cluster with one to three clusters per stem. As flowers age they turn to a deep purple. **Fruit** is about ¾" long with wings often tinged purple. **Blooms** April to June. **Occurs** throughout Utah to Colorado, Arizona, and New Mexico. Found in desert scrub, sagebrush, pinyon juniper, and ponderosa pine communities. (3,600 to 9,000 ft)

COMMENTS: Found throughout Capitol Reef, most commonly along the Cathedral Valley Loop drive in early spring. It also occurs in Arches, Canyonlands, Bryce Canyon, Bears Ears, Glen Canyon, Grand Staircase, and Zion.

Synonyms: Cymopterus purpureus, Epallageiton purpureum

PINNATE SPRING PARSLEY

Cymopterus beckii | **Carrot Family** Apiaceae

A bright green herbaceous perennial that reaches 16" in height. **Leaves** extend up the stems from a base covered with dried, old brownish leaf bases. Leaves are up to 4" long, once to twice pinnately compound, with two to three pairs of lateral leaflets. Leaflets are linear to linear elliptic, ¼" to 1½" long (terminal leaflet may be slightly longer), and ⅛" wide. The leaves give the plant a feathery looking appearance. Flowering stalk is usually 4" tall but may extend 8" if stretching for the light or in a good year. Yellow **flowers** are borne in a flat-topped cluster, with one to three clusters per stem. Fruit is about ¼" long, oblong in shape with wings. **Blooms** early May to early August. **Occurs** in south central Utah and from a single location in Arizona. Found in sandy soils or cracks in sandstone within Navajo, Kayenta, Wingate, or rarely Cutler formations in pinyon juniper, ponderosa pine, Douglas fir, or high mountain brush communities. (5,500 to 8,000 ft)

COMMENTS: The type locality is within Capitol Reef. This is an endemic and National Park Service sensitive species being closely monitored within Capitol Reef.

RUSH LOMATIUM

Lomatium junceum | **Carrot Family** Apiaceae

An herbaceous perennial that appears as a rounded, broom like clump. It grows to 15" tall from a woody base that is covered with persistent leaf stalks. Plants die back in the winter but the old leaves remain and turn golden yellow. New growth sprouts up among these dry golden leaves. All **leaves** are basal, rarely branching. Leaves divide into sessile leaflets that are usually continuous with the main leaf. Leaflets are linear and less than ⅛" in width. Each leaf has seven or fewer round, elongated leaflets. **Flower** umbels have six to 13 rays with yellow petals and stamens. Flower color fades to white as they dry. Calyx teeth are greenish, acute shaped and about 1/16" in length. **Fruits** are up to ⅜" long, about ⅛" wide, with lateral wings. **Blooms** in May. **Occurs** only in south central Utah. Found in mixed desert scrub, sagebrush, pinyon juniper, and ponderosa pine communities. (5,300 to 8,200 ft)

COMMENTS: This is an endemic species found from the San Rafael Swell in central Utah south to the Waterpocket Fold within Capitol Reef. It is found on the Moenkopi formation in the central and northern portions of Capitol Reef. This is a National Park Service sensitive species.

Synonyms: Aletes juncea

EASTWOOD'S MILKWEED

Asclepias macrosperma | **Dogbane Family** Apocynaceae

A small, low-growing herbaceous perennial with few, mostly unbranched, sprawling **stems**. Both stems and leaves are covered with tiny white matted hairs, giving the plant a grayish green appearance. Opposite **leaves** are broadly oval to lance shaped, ¾" to 2½" long, and ½" to ¾" wide. Leaves are often slightly folded in half lengthwise. Small pale yellow to greenish **flowers** bloom from branch tips. **Seed** capsules are broadly spindle shaped, on short pedicels, 1¼" to 2½" long and ½" wide, with slightly hairy to smooth surfaces. **Blooms** late April to early July. **Occurs** in central and southern Utah and Arizona. Found in mixed desert scrub, sagebrush, and pinyon juniper communities. (3,200 to 6,500 feet)

COMMENTS: It typically grows in dry, sandy soils on hills, benches, or bottomlands and is found in the southern portions of Capitol Reef. It also occurs in Arches, Grand Staircase, and Canyonlands.

Synonyms: Asclepias involucrata var. tomentosa

VISCID RABBITBRUSH

Chrysothamnus viscidiflorus | **Sunflower Family** Asteraceae

A low to moderate-sized perennial shrub up to 40" in height, but usually closer to 18" to 24" tall. **Stems** are green, tan or whitish in color depending on the variety. Alternate **leaves** are ½" to 1" long, linear to oblong. They may be one to five nerved. Numerous yellow **flowers** bloom in terminal flower heads. **Seeds** are inconspicuous. **Blooms** July to October. **Occurs** throughout the western United States to Canada and south to Mexico. It typically grows in dry, sandy soils on hills, benches, and occasionally in washes; found in desert scrub, sagebrush, blackbrush, and pinyon juniper woodland communities. (2,200 to 9,000 ft)

COMMENTS: Common throughout Capitol Reef. It also occurs in Arches, Canyonlands, Bryce Canyon, Bears Ears, Glen Canyon, and Zion.

Synonyms: Chrysothamnus glaucus, Chrysothamnus pumilus var. acuminatus , Chrysothamnus pumilus var. latus , Chrysothamnus stenolepis

NAKED STEM SUNRAYS

Enceliopsis nudicaulis | **Sunflower Family** Asteraceae

An herbaceous perennial up to 20" tall, with a woody taproot. Plant is leafy only at the base, with a long naked **stem** supporting each flower head. Stems and leaves are gray-green in color. Entire **leaves** are up to 3" long and equally wide, covered in dense gray woolly hairs, oval to round in shape, and grow on a stalk. Large yellow **flower heads** are solitary on long stems; entire head is about 2" across. Receptacle and **seeds** together become a tawny yellow, globe shaped ball. **Blooms** mid April to July. **Occurs** throughout Utah, Nevada, Arizona, and California. It typically grows in clay or gypsiferous soils, in blackbrush, mixed desert scrub, and pinyon juniper communities. (2,300 to 7,000 ft)

COMMENTS: Common in the central portion of Capitol Reef, most often seen along Highway 24 east of the Visitor Center, near Chimney Rock, and along the scenic drive. It also occurs in Arches, Canyonlands, and Glen Canyon. The specific name, *nudicaulis,* refers to the long bare stem that bears each flower head.

Synonyms: Enceliopsis tuta

RUBBER RABBITBRUSH

Ericameria nauseosa | **Sunflower Family** Asteraceae

A perennial shrub that grows up to 6' tall from a single rootstalk. Branches are generally all upright and fairly parallel, giving the plant a somewhat broomlike appearance. **Stems** are grayish in color, typically covered with dense, woolly, matted hairs and glands. New stem growth appears green. Alternate **leaves** are ¾" to 4" long, very narrow, linear, and three-nerved. They may be covered with fine hairs. Numerous yellow **flowers** bloom in terminal flower heads. **Seed**s are inconspicuous. **Blooms** August to October. **Occurs** throughout the western United States to Canada and south to Mexico. It typically grows in dry, sandy soils on hills, benches and occasionally in washes; found in desert scrub, sagebrush, and pinyon juniper woodland communities. It also grows along washes forming dense stands of this single species. It is frequently seen in disturbed or heavily grazed sites. (2,200 to 9,000 ft)

COMMENTS: Common throughout Capitol Reef. It also occurs in Glen Canyon. There are numerous varieties of this species. *Nauseosa* refers to the strong, acrid scent of these plants. Rubbery latex can be made from the sap of this plant and flowers produce a yellow dye. Several American Indian groups used rabbitbrush medicinally, including as treatment for colds and coughs. Another common name for this plant is "chamise."

Synonyms: Chrysothamnus nauseosus, Chrysothamnus pallidus

RAYLESS SHAGGY FLEABANE

Erigeron aphanactis | **Sunflower Family** Asteraceae

A perennial ranging from 2" to 8" in height, with numerous short branches arising from a single base. **Stems** may be upright or sprawl along the ground. Stems and leaves are usually covered with stiff hairs. Basal **leaves** are narrow and lance or spatula shaped, up to 3" long. Leaves are entire with the upper ones becoming smaller and smaller. **Disk flowers** are most prominent and bright yellow. Flower head is about ½" wide and tall. **Seeds** are inconspicuous. **Blooms** May to July. **Occurs** from Oregon south to California and Arizona, and east to Utah and Colorado. It typically grows in clay soils in desert scrub, sagebrush, and pinyon juniper communities. (4,300 to 8,800 ft)

COMMENTS: Most commonly seen in the central portion of Capitol Reef, and in Arches, Bryce Canyon, Bears Ears, and Canyonlands.

SAND-DUNE WALLFLOWER

Erysimum capitatum | **Mustard Family** Brassicaceae

A biennial or short-lived perennial with one to many stems that may reach 3' in height. Gray-green **leaves** (up to 4" long and ¼ to ½" wide) grow along the stem and are linear to lance shaped. Large, older plants may have spatula-shaped leaves near the base. **Flowers** grow in dense, rounded clusters at the top of each stem. Individual flowers are ½" to 1" across. Flowers are typically yellow to orange, but may also be creamy white to lavender in color. **Seed pods** are long, narrow, and slightly flattened capsules that grow upwards rather than drooping down. **Blooms** March to September. **Occurs** throughout much of the western U.S. and north into Canada. Found in desert scrub, pinyon-juniper, ponderosa pine, Douglas Fir to spruce forests. (2,500 to 12,000 ft)

COMMENTS: This wallflower is distinguished from others of this genus by having petals longer than ½". It can be seen in Bears Ears, Canyonlands, Bryce Canyon, Zion, Glen Canyon, and Arches, but hasn't been recorded in Capitol Reef to date. Native Americans use the plant to treat tuberculosis and headaches. Navajos ground seeds into a flour, then toasted them over a fire for use in soups or stews. Botanical authorities have assigned different names to this species and split it into numerous varieties, suggesting a high degree of variability of this plant throughout its range.

HOPI BLANKETFLOWER

Gaillardia pinnatifida | **Sunflower Family** Asteraceae

An herbaceous perennial that grows 20" tall. **Leaves** are ⅜" to 2¾" long and 1/16" to ⅝" wide, lobed, or occasionally entire, elliptic in shape, and have spiny hairs along their edges. Leaves grow on short stalks and occur only on the lower half of the stem or sometimes only basally. **Ray flowers** are yellow; **disk** flowers are purple or green purplish, ¾" to 1½" across. Flower heads are solitary on stems. Tiny **seeds** are covered with white woolly hairs. **Blooms** mid April to August. **Occurs** in eastern and southern Utah, Colorado, Arizona, and Texas south into Mexico. It typically grows in shallow, sandy soils on rocky benches in desert scrub and pinyon juniper woodlands. (2,800 to 7,000 ft)

COMMENTS: Found primarily south of Fruita in Capitol Reef. It also occurs in Arches, Canyonlands, Glen Canyon, and Zion. Hopi Indians reportedly used this species as a diuretic,and Navajo Indians used it as remedy for gout.

Synonyms: Gaillardia crassifolia

BASIN BLANKETFLOWER

Gaillardia spathulata | **Sunflower Family** Asteraceae

An herbaceous perennial that grows to about 14" tall. Plant is generally leafy to at least halfway up the stalk. **Leaves** are 3⁄8" to 3" long and up to 1" wide, entire, or toothed, oval to elliptic in shape, and grow either directly from the stem or on short stalks. Leaves are sparsely covered with long shaggy hairs and glands. Yellow **flower heads** are solitary on the stem, about 1¼" to 2" across. Receptacle and **seeds** together become a tawny yellow, globe-shaped ball. Tiny individual seeds are covered with yellow woolly hairs. **Blooms** mid April to November. **Occurs** in eastern and southern Utah. It typically grows in sandy soils in rocky washes or bottomlands in mixed desert scrub. (3,900 to 7,700 ft)

COMMENTS: This endemic species is fairly common in the central and southern portions of Capitol Reef, and abundant in Grand Wash. It also occurs in Arches, Grand Staircase, and Canyonlands. The specific name, *spathulata*, means "spoon shaped," referring to its leaves. The type locality is Rabbit Valley, just west of Capitol Reef National Park. American Indians have several medicinal uses for species within this genus.

CURLY CUP GUMWEED

Grindelia squarrosa | **Sunflower Family** Asteraceae

An erect, herbaceous perennial that reaches 28" in height. **Leaves** are ¾" to 2" long and ½" to ¾" wide, entire or irregularly toothed and oblong in shape. Upper leaves often clasp the stem. **Stems** and leaves are covered with sticky glands, hence the name gumweed. Yellow **flowerheads** are solitary on the stems; each flower head is about ½" across. The flower head sits in a cup shaped receptacle surrounded by numerous green **bracts**. These bracts are strongly curved downwards and covered with sticky glands. Numerous tiny **seeds** form in the receptacle, each with several hairs attached to one end. **Blooms** July to November. **Occurs** throughout Utah, Wyoming to New Mexico and Arizona. It typically grows in sandy soils in disturbed sites. (4,300 to 7,000 ft)

COMMENTS: Fairly common in the orchards and pastures in the central portion of Capitol Reef. It also occurs in Bryce Canyon, Arches, Canyonlands, and Zion. American Indians and early pioneers used plants in this genus for treating breathing problems.

Synonyms: Grindelia arguta

BROOM SNAKEWEED

Gutierrezia sarothrae | **Sunflower Family** Asteraceae

A rounded, perennial shrub that grows from a single rootstalk with upright branches that give the plant a somewhat broomlike appearance. Shrubs reach 12" to 20" in height. **Stems** are slender, older stems are grayish to tan in color, and new growth is green. **Leaves** on the branches are ¾" to 2¾" long and about 1⁄16" wide, linear, and threadlike. Leaves reduce in size upward on the stems. Four tiny, yellow **flowers** bloom in each flower head. Typically three to eight flower heads group together at branch tips. Flowers tend to be cone shaped rather than cylindrical. **Seeds** are inconspicuous. **Blooms** July to November. **Occurs** widespread throughout western United States to Canada and south to Mexico. Typically found in dry, sandy soils on hills, benches, and occasionally in washes in mixed desert scrub, sagebrush, rabbitbrush, and pinyon juniper woodland communities. Often found in disturbed or heavily grazed sites. (2,800 to 6,000 ft)

COMMENTS: Common throughout Capitol Reef and all the Southern Utah parks. This species is often confused with its close relative, *G. microcephala*, Thread snakeweed. Key differences between these two species are the more numerous flowers per head and cone shaped flower heads in this snakeweed. Plants are poisonous to livestock.

Synonyms: Brachyris divaricata, Gutierrezia divaricata, Gutierrezia diversifolia,Gutierrezia tenuis, Solidago sarothrae

COMMON SUNFLOWER

Helianthus annuus | **Sunflower Family** Asteraceae

An annual with simple branches that grows to 16" tall. Plant is covered with short, stiff hairs that give it a rough feeling when touched. Alternate **leaves** are 2" to 12" long and ¾" to 12" wide, toothed, and oval to egg shaped with squared off or heart shaped bases. Leaves all grow on short stalks and are covered with stiff hairs. **Flower heads** are typically solitary on the stem ends; each flower head is about 2" to 4" across. Ray flowers are yellow. The central disk flowers tend to be red to dark purple/brown in color. Tiny individual **seeds** are covered with white, woolly hairs. **Blooms** June to September. **Occurs** throughout Utah and most of the western United States, north to Canada, and south to Mexico. Typically found in sandy soils of mixed desert scrub, saltbush, and pinyon juniper woodland communities. Often found in disturbed sites. (3,900 to 8,000 ft)

COMMENTS: Most often seen along roadsides, in orchards and pastures in the central portion of Capitol Reef. It also occurs in Arches, Bryce Canyon, Canyonlands, Bears Ears, Glen Canyon, and Zion. This species has a long history of use by American Indians as a food plant. It is cultivated and harvested today for birdseed.

Synonyms: Helianthus lenticularis

HAIRY GOLDENASTER

Heterotheca villosa var. villosa | **Sunflower Family** Asteraceae

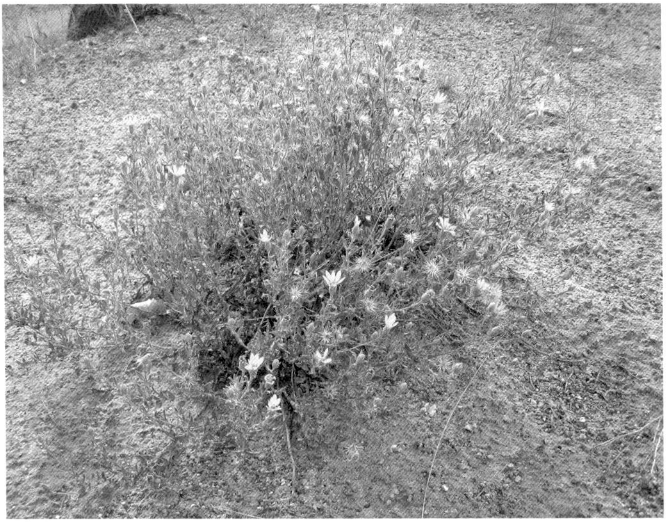

An herbaceous perennial that ranges from 7" to 20" tall. It forms a scraggly clump with many sprawling **stems**. Foliage is covered with soft hairs and occasionally with glands. Gray-green to green **leaves** are 2/3" to 2" long, entire, and elliptical to spatula shaped. Yellow **flower heads** are multiple per stalk, each about ½" across, with ten to twenty-five ray flowers, and yellow disk flowers. **Seeds** have hairy bristles. **Blooms** May to September. **Occurs** throughout Utah and the western United States. Typically found in mixed desert scrub, sagebrush, pinyon juniper woodland, ponderosa pine, and aspen communities. (3,600 to 9,100 ft)

COMMENTS: Found widespread throughout Capitol Reef on dry hills and benches, and in Glen Canyon and Grand Staircase. The specific name, *villosa*, refers to the soft, gray hairs covering the foliage. This species is a part of the complex group of plants that have received various taxonomic treatments over the years. It is a common wildflower throughout the West.

Synonyms: Chrysopsis mollis, Chrysopsis villosa, Chrysopsis villosa var. villosa

FINELEAF WOOLLYWHITE OR TELEGRAPH FLOWER

Hymenopappus filifolius | **Sunflower Family** Asteraceae

An herbaceous perennial that grows up to 24" tall. **Stems** and leaves are covered with grayish white felt-like hairs, giving the plant a grayish appearance. Basal **leaves** (2" to 8" long) are larger than stem leaves; all are divided twice into narrow threadlike segments. One to two tiny yellow **flower heads** grow on each stem (¼" across) and consist only of disk flowers with elongated stamens. Tiny **seeds** are densely hairy and up to ¼" long. **Blooms** May to August. **Occurs** throughout Utah, Colorado, Arizona, New Mexico, and Texas. Grows in sandy soils throughout a wide variety of landforms in mixed desert scrub, sagebrush, pinyon juniper woodland, and ponderosa pine forests. (3,500 to 8,900 ft)

COMMENTS: Fairly common throughout Capitol Reef. It also occurs in Arches, Canyonlands, Bryce Canyon, Bears Ears, Cedar Breaks, Glen Canyon, Grand Staircase, and Zion. This is a highly variable species that botanists from different states treat differently as to species and varieties. The specific name for this species, *filifolius*, means "threadleaf."

COLORADO RUBBERWEED

Hymenoxys richardsonii | **Sunflower Family** Asteraceae

An herbaceous perennial that grows from a multi-branched, woody rootstalk. Plants are 4" to 16" in height. **Stems** arising from the base are covered with dry, brown leaf bases from previous year's growth. Green **leaves** are ¾" to 4¾" long, divided into three to five (sometimes seven) leaflets, and are linear. Foliage is usually hairy, but may be smooth and hairless. Yellow **flower heads** bloom in an open terminal cluster. Each flower head is about ¾" to 1" across. Tiny **seeds** about ⅛" long are covered with fine hairs. **Blooms** June to August. **Occurs** throughout Utah, north to Canada, and south to Arizona. Typically found in dry, sandy to rocky soils on hills and benches in mixed desert scrub, sagebrush, pinyon juniper woodland, ponderosa pine, aspen, and fir communities. (4,800 to 10,000 ft)

COMMENTS: Common throughout the northern and central portions of Capitol Reef. It also occurs in Bryce Canyon, Glen Canyon, Grand Staircase, and Canyonlands. Plants are poisonous to livestock.

Synonyms: Actinella richardsonii

DESERT DANDELION

Malacothrix sonchoides | **Sunflower Family** Asteraceae

An annual that grows 2" to 14" tall. Plant grows a basal rosette of toothed leaves with a fairly naked **stem** topped with a large yellow flower head. Toothed **leaves** (up to 4½" long and 1" wide) form a basal rosette flattened on the ground. Few leaves grow up the stem. Yellow **flower heads** are solitary or few to a cluster; entire flower head is about 1" wide. Receptacle and **seeds** become a whitish, soft bristly ball. **Blooms** mid April to June. **Occurs** throughout Utah into Nevada, New Mexico, Nebraska, and California. Found in sandy soils, in blackbrush, desert scrub, sagebrush, and pinyon juniper woodland communities. (3,000 to 6,100 ft)

COMMENTS: Found in the southern portion of Capitol Reef, most often seen on the route to Halls Creek Narrows. It also occurs in Arches, Glen Canyon, Grand Staircase, and Canyonlands. The genus name, *Malacothrix,* comes from the Greek *malakos,* meaning "soft" and *thrix,* meaning "hairs," thus referring to the soft bristles on the seeds.

Synonyms: Leptoseris sonchoides, Malacothrix runcinata

LOBELEAF GROUNDSEL

Packera multilobata | **Sunflower Family** Asteraceae

An herbaceous perennial that grows 4" to 24" tall. Plants appear as a basal clump of green leaves with flower stalks extending above the clump. **Leaves** are primarily basal, ¾" to 4¾" long and up to 1⅓" wide, egg to spatula shaped, and deeply lobed. Leaves on the stems are much reduced upwards. Bright yellow **flower heads** are borne in flat-topped clusters; about ⅜" to 1" across. There are usually seven to 13 ray flowers and the central disk flowers are also yellow. **Seeds** are tiny with white hairs. **Blooms** mid April to August. **Occurs** throughout Utah, and much of the western United States. Found on dry slopes in sandy to limestone soils of mixed desert scrub, sagebrush, pinyon juniper woodland, ponderosa pine, and lodgepole pine communities (3,000 to 11,200 ft)

COMMENTS: Common throughout Capitol Reef, and in Glen Canyon and Grand Staircase. The specific name, *multilobata*, refers to the deeply lobed leaves.

Synonyms: Senecio multilobatus, Senecio lynceus, Senecio prolixus, Senecio stygius, Senecio thornberi, Senecio uintahensis

GREENSTEM PAPERFLOWER

Psilotrophe sparsiflora | **Sunflower Family** Asteraceae

An herbaceous perennial that grows from a branched, woody rootstalk. Plants are 6" to 24" tall, bushy and scraggly looking. As the name implies, **stems** are greenish, and usually covered with fine woolly hairs. **Leaves** are 3/8" to 4½" long, 1/16" to 3/8" wide, and spatula shaped. Yellow **flower heads** usually have only three petals that droop downwards. Each flower head is about 1" across. **Seeds** are inconspicuous. **Blooms** May to July. **Occurs** in southern Utah, south to Arizona, New Mexico, and Mexico. It typically grows in dry, sandy to rocky soils on hills and benches; found in mixed desert scrub, sagebrush, and pinyon juniper woodland communities. (4,700 to 6,700 ft)

COMMENTS: Common throughout the northern and central portions of Capitol Reef. It also occurs in Bryce Canyon, Grand Staircase, and Glen Canyon. Plants are poisonous to livestock.

Synonyms: Riddellia tagetina var. sparsiflora

ROUGH MULES EARS

Scabrethia scabra | **Sunflower Family** Asteraceae

A moderate to large perennial shrub that tends to grow in dense, green clumps. Entire **leaves** (up to 7" long and 1" wide) are bright green, rough to touch, and linear in shape. Large yellow **flower heads** are up to 3" wide and tend to be solitary on the stem ends. The plant often blooms profusely covering the entire shrub with flowers. The receptacle forms a dark brown hard, bristly ball that contains the small, black, or dark brown **seeds**. **Blooms** May to August. **Occurs** throughout Utah into New Mexico, Arizona, Colorado, and Wyoming. Found in sandy soils of blackbrush, desert scrub, oak, ponderosa pine, and pinyon juniper woodland communities. (4,000 to 8,500 ft)

COMMENTS: Found throughout Capitol Reef, Grand Staircase, and Glen Canyon, most often in washes. The specific name, *scabra*, refers to the rough surface of the leaves.

Synonyms: Wyethia scabra

THRIFTY GOLDENWEED

Stenotus armerioides var. armerioides | **Sunflower Family** Asteraceae

An herbaceous perennial that grows in dense clumps from a woody taproot. Plants are generally 2" to 8" tall. **Stems** arising from a basal clump are covered with dry, brown leaf bases from previous year's growth. Dark green basal **leaves** are ½" to 3" long, entire, linear and covered with resinous glands. Leaves on the stems are few and much reduced. Yellow **flower heads** are solitary, each about ¾" across, with ten to 12 ray flowers and numerous dark brown disk flowers. **Seeds** are inconspicuous. **Blooms** May to July. **Occurs** in central and southern Utah, Montana, Nebraska, and south to Arizona. Typically found on dry slopes or rocky ridges in mixed desert scrub, sagebrush, blackbrush, pinyon juniper, and ponderosa pine woodland communities. (3,900 to 7,900 ft)

COMMENTS: Most commonly seen in the central and southern portions of Capitol Reef, particularly in Spring Canyon and Capitol Gorge. It also occurs in Glen Canyon, Grand Staircase, and Canyonlands.

Synonyms: Haplopappus armerioides

SPINELESS HORSEBRUSH

Tetradymia canescens | **Sunflower Family** Asteraceae

A moderate sized, intricate branching, and rounded shrub that grows to 2' tall. **Stems** are grayish, not spiny but covered with soft hairs. Older stems lose their woolliness and become smooth and gray, the bark eventually shredding in strips. **Leaves** are gray-green to green, linear, straight, up to 1½" long, and may or may not be densely covered with hairs. **Flower heads** are light yellow, and clustered at the ends of branches. **Seeds** are inconspicuous. **Blooms** June to September. **Occurs** throughout Utah and the western United States. Found in sagebrush, mixed desert scrub, desert grasslands, ponderosa pine, and aspen woodlands. (5,000 to 10,300 ft)

COMMENTS: Found in the northern and central portions of Capitol Reef. It also occurs in Arches, Bryce Canyon, Canyonlands, Cedar Breaks, Glen Canyon, and Zion. Hopi people use the leaves and roots for medicinal purposes. It is toxic to domestic sheep and can cause their death, however, does not seem to affect cattle.

Synonyms: Tetradymia canescens var. inermis

STEMLESS WOOLLYBASE

Tetraneuris acaulis | **Sunflower Family** Asteraceae

An herbaceous perennial that grows in short, stemless clumps. Plants without the flowering stalk are about 2" to 3" tall. Plant base is covered with dry, dark brown leaf bases from previous year's growth. New **leaves** are bright green, 1/16" to 2½" long, linear, threadlike, and often covered with soft woolly hairs. Flower heads are borne on a stalk up to 12" tall. Yellow **flower heads** are about 1" to 1½" across. **Seeds** are inconspicuous. **Blooms** May to July. **Occurs** throughout central and southern Utah, Colorado, and Arizona. Found in dry, sandy soils on hills and benches in mixed desert scrub, sagebrush, and pinyon juniper woodland communities. (3,700 to 8,200 ft)

COMMENTS: Can be seen throughout Capitol Reef. This species has several varieties, three of which occur in the Capitol Reef area, so you'll see some variation in plants depending on which variety you find. This species also occurs in Arches, Bryce Canyon, Canyonlands, Bears Ears, Grand Staircase, and Zion.

Synonyms: Actinella eradiata, Hymenoxys acaulis

LOW HYMENOXYS

Tetraneuris acaulis var. arizonica | **Sunflower Family** Asteraceae

A tiny mound-shaped perennial rarely more than 3" tall. Base of plant is covered with short brownish or blackish shredding leaf bases. Plants have no **stems**. **Leaves** are up to 2/3" long, 1/8" wide, bright green, and linear. The leafless flowering stalk is up to 2/3" tall. **Flower heads** are usually solitary and sessile or nearly so amongst the tufts of basal leaves. Ray flowers are yellow, about 2/3" wide. **Seeds** are inconspicuous. **Blooms** May to June. **Occurs** in south central Utah. Found in pinyon juniper woodland, sagebrush, mixed desert scrub, ponderosa pine, and bristlecone pine communities. (4,400 to 8,600 ft)

COMMENTS: This variety includes *T. acaulis var. nana* which is a National Park Service sensitive species. It is found in the northern portions of Capitol Reef. Plants found in Capitol Reef are more caespitose with flower heads nestled down completely amongst the leaves. Further work is needed to confirm the status of this variety.

Synonyms: Actinea acaulis var. arizonica, Hymenoxys acaulis var. arizonica, Hymenoxys acaulis var. nana, Tetraneuris acaulis var. nana, Tetraneuris arizonica

HOPI TEA GREENTHREAD

Thelesperma megapotamicum | **Sunflower Family** Asteraceae

An herbaceous perennial that grows 11" to 30" tall, with a stout rootstalk. Plant appears as a basal clump of green leaves with a flower stalk extending above the clump. **Leaves** are primarily basal, up to 2¾" long, and once to twice divided with linear lobes. Bright yellow **flower heads** form on the terminal end of a naked stem, are typically solitary, and the entire flower head is about ½" wide and ½" tall. Central disk flowers are yellow. Ray flowers are lacking. **Seeds** are inconspicuous. **Blooms** May to October. **Occurs** in southern and central Utah, Wyoming, Nebraska, to Arizona, New Mexico, and south into Mexico and South America. Found in fine sandy soils of mixed desert scrub to ponderosa pine communities. (3,000 to 7,500 ft)

COMMENTS: This species is found just east of Capitol Reef and likely occurs in the southern portion of the Park. It also occurs in Canyonlands, Glen Canyon, and Zion. Ancestral Puebloans used plants in this genus for medicinal purposes. A refreshing "spearmint" flavored tea made from this genus is a traditional drink of New Mexicans of Spanish decent. Hopi people also make a dye from these plants to color basketry and textiles.

Synonyms: Tetradymia canescens var. inermis

GREENTHREAD

Thelesperma subnudum | **Sunflower Family** Asteraceae

An herbaceous perennial that grows 1" to 14" tall. Plants appear as a basal clump of green leaves with a flower stalk extending above the clump. **Leaves** are primarily basal, ½" to 3" long and about 1/16" to 1/8" wide, and narrowly linear. Leaves may be entire or lobed. Bright yellow **flower heads** are typically solitary on the stem ends; entire flower head is about 1" across. Central disk flowers are also yellow. The green receptacle is smooth, shiny, and always has a "crown" of **bracts** extending just below the ray flowers. **Seeds** are inconspicuous. **Blooms** mid April to August. **Occurs** throughout much of Utah, Colorado, Arizona, and New Mexico. Found in fine sandy to clay soils of mixed desert scrub, saltbush, and pinyon juniper communities. (3,500 to 8,000 ft)

COMMENTS: Common throughout Capitol Reef, and Arches, Canyonlands, Grand Staircase, and Glen Canyon. Ancestral Puebloans used plants in this genus for medicinal purposes. A refreshing "spearmint" flavored tea made from this genus is a traditional drink of New Mexico.

Synonyms: Thelesperma pubescens var. caespitosum,Thelesperma s ubnudum var. pubescens

ALPINE GREENTHREAD

Thelesperma windhamii | **Sunflower Family** Asteraceae

An herbaceous perennial ranging from ¾" to 2¾" tall that grows from a taproot. **Leaves** are mainly at base of the stem, ½" to 1¼" long, some or all leaves are lobed, and resemble a tiny turkey's foot. **Flower heads** contain only disk flowers, are bright yellow, and about ¼" broad. **Blooms** late June to July. **Occurs** only in south central Utah. Found in pinyon juniper, open ponderosa pine, mountain scrub, and bristlecone pine communities. (7,300 to 9,000 ft)

COMMENTS: The dwarf size and lack of ray flowers make this species easy to differentiate from other *Thelesperma*. This is an endemic National Park Service sensitive species, typically found in the northern portion of Capitol Reef.

LAST CHANCE TOWNSENDIA

Townsendia aprica | **Sunflower Family** Asteraceae

An herbaceous perennial no more than 1" tall that grows as a tiny mound. **Leaves** grow in a rosette (3/8" to ½" long and 1/16" to 1/8" wide). They are spatula to lance shaped and entire. Yellow ray **flowers** have a purplish vein on the underside, which is diagnostic for this species. Flower heads are ½" to ¾" across and sessile amongst the leaf rosettes. Tiny **seeds** covered with white fluffy hairs resemble a small dandelion seed ball. **Blooms** April to May. **Occurs** only in central Utah. It typically grows in clay soils on hills and benches in desert scrub, and pinyon juniper woodland communities. (6,100 to 8,000 ft)

COMMENTS: Found in the northern portions of Capitol Reef. This endemic species is federally listed as a threatened species and is protected throughout its range.

RAYLESS TANSYASTER

Xanthisma grindelioides | **Sunflower Family** Asteraceae

A small perennial shrub that grows up to 12" tall from a stout taproot. Foliage is covered with short, spreading, glandular hairs. Plant base tends to be covered with dark brown dried leaves from previous years' growth. **Leaves** on the stems are up to 1¾" long and about ½" wide, spatula to lance shaped, with the attachment at the narrow end of the leaf. Leaf margins are toothed with spiny tips on each tooth. Leaves on the stems may be reduced upwards or lacking. **Flower heads** may be solitary or in a terminal cluster, and are about 1/3" long and ½" wide. There are no ray flowers or what are commonly called the petals. Floral bracts are green or brown. **Seeds** are inconspicuous. **Blooms** May to August. **Occurs** throughout Utah to Nevada, Arizona, and New Mexico. Found in mixed desert scrub, sagebrush, and pinyon juniper woodland communities. (4,400 to 10,400 ft)

COMMENTS: Found in the central and southern portions of Capitol Reef, and in Glen Canyon, and Grand Staircase. There are two varieties of this species. One is a Great Basin endemic, and the other variety occurs throughout Capitol Reef and the western United States. The genus name, *Xanthisma,* is Greek, meaning "that which is dyed yellow."

Synonyms: Eriocarpum grindelioides, Haplopappus nuttallii, Machaeranthera grindelioides

FREMONT'S BARBERRY

Berberis fremontii | **Barberry Family** Berberidaceae

An intricately **branching**, large shrub that grows up to 7' tall and often as broad. This is a stout, spiny shrub that you don't want to walk through. Compound **leaves** are up to 4⅓" long with three to nine leaflets that grow in clusters along the branches. Leaves are holly shaped and spiny. Leaflets typically have five-toothed lobes, ½" to 1¼" long, and ⅛" to 1¼" wide. Both surfaces of the leaves are smooth; the upper surface is a shiny, dark green. Showy yellow **flowers** grow in clusters; petals are ⅜" to ⅝" long with rounded tips. **Berries** are purplish, borne in grape like clusters. **Blooms** April to July. **Occurs** in Southern Utah, Arizona, and New Mexico. It typically grows in canyon bottoms or on side slopes in desert scrub and pinyon juniper woodland. (3,000 to 7,700 ft)

COMMENTS: It is common throughout Capitol Reef, but particularly abundant and showy in Grand Wash and Capitol Gorge. It also occurs in Glen Canyon and Grand Staircase. The roots of these plants have several medicinal properties, most commonly used as a laxative, fever reducer, and for wound cleaning. The specific name, *fremontii*, is for John C. Fremont, an early explorer in the southwest.

Synonyms: Mahonia fremontii, Odostemon fremontii

YELLOW CATSPAW

Cryptantha flava | **Borage Family** Boraginaceae

An herbaceous perennial that grows from 5" to 15" tall, typically to about 10". Numerous **stems** and leaves are covered with stiff hairs. Narrow **leaves** are entire, linear, ¾" to 3½" long and ⅛" to ¼" wide. The underside of each leaf is covered with bristly hairs that have blisters or pustules at the base of each hair. Yellow **flowers** grow in a narrow flower cluster 2" to 8" long. The yellow corolla tube is about ⅜" long, with little or no crests at the base. Fornices are yellow and blunt-ended. **Nutlets** (one to two) are smooth and glossy. **Blooms** mid April to July. **Occurs** throughout much of Utah, Colorado, Wyoming, New Mexico, and Arizona. Associated with saltbush scrub, mixed desert scrub, and pinyon juniper woodland communities, typically on hillsides and uplands of barren clay soils. (5,700 to 9,200 ft)

COMMENTS: Common throughout Capitol Reef, and in Arches, Bryce Canyon, Bears Ears, Canyonlands, Grand Staircase,and Glen Canyon.

Synonyms: Oreocarya flava

SHOWY STONESEED

Lithospermum incisum | **Borage Family** Boraginaceae

An herbaceous perennial that grows to 20" tall, but more often seen about 10" tall. Plants often have multiple stems. **Stems** and leaves are covered with short, stiff hairs. Narrow **leaves** are entire, linear, ⅜" to 2" long. Yellow **flowers** grow along an unbranched, elongated stalk with the lowermost flowers blooming first. Flowers have a rather long tube, ⅜" to 1 1/8" long, with the petals spreading widely at the top and appearing wrinkled or crinkly and delicate. **Nutlets** are hard and shiny. **Blooms** April to July. **Occurs** throughout Utah, Canada, to Mexico. Found in mixed desert scrub, sagebrush, and pinyon juniper woodland communities. (4,400 to 9,400 ft)

COMMENTS: Another common name for this genus is "Puccoon." The name *Lithospermum* is derived from the Greek word *lithos*, which means "stone," and *sperm*, which means "seed," hence the common name "Stoneseed." American Indians had several medicinal uses for the roots and leaves. Roots were also used to make a red-violet dye. Mostly commonly seen in the central and southern portions of Capitol Reef, and in Arches, Bryce Canyon, Canyonlands, Bears Ears, Glen Canyon, Cedar Breaks, Grand Staircase, and Zion.

Synonyms: Batschia linearifolia, Lithospermum angustifolium, Lithospermum linearifolium, Lithospermum mandanense

PRETTY STONESEED

Lithospermum multiflorum | **Borage Family** Boraginaceae

An herbaceous perennial, often with diversely branching stems that give it a tufted appearance. Typically grows 12" to 14" tall. **Stems** and leaves are covered with short, stiff hairs. Narrow linear **leaves** are entire, ¾" to 2⅜" long with short, stiff hairs on the upper surface and often with longer hairs on the underside. Leaves become smaller on the upper stems and appear as bracts below the flowers. Yellow orange **flowers** grow along an unbranched stalk with the lowermost flowers blooming first. Flowers are rather small and funnel shaped, the corolla tube being only about 3/8" long. Petals spread widely at the top of the tube. **Nutlets**, typically three, are white, hard and shiny. **Blooms** June to August. **Occurs** in southern Utah Colorado, Arizona, Texas, and northern Mexico. Found in sagebrush to pinyon juniper woodland, and ponderosa pine communities. (6,000 to 9,600 ft)

COMMENTS: The roots contain a deep red dye used by American Indians. Found in the higher elevation, northern portion of Capitol Reef, and in Bryce Canyon, Cedar Breaks, and Zion.

RYDBERG'S TWINPOD

Physaria acutifolia | **Mustard Family** Brassicaceae

An herbaceous perennial that forms a low clump of dull greenish-blue leaves close to the ground. Without the flowering stalk the clump is usually 2" to 4" tall. The rootstalk is usually covered with dry, brown leaves remaining from previous years' growth. **Stems** may be erect or sprawling along the ground. The most obvious **leaves** are basal, 5/8" to 3½" long and ¼" to 1¾" wide, and entire or sometimes angular. Leaves along the stems are greatly reduced in size. Flowering stalk is usually ¼" to 5/8" long, topped with bright yellow **flowers**. **Seedpods** are ball shaped, inflated, and typically with two pods joined along the top, hence the common name, twinpod. **Blooms** mid April to July. **Occurs** throughout Utah to Colorado, and Wyoming. Found in mixed desert scrub, sagebrush, pinyon juniper woodland, ponderosa pine, and spruce fir communities. (3,700 to 11,200 feet)

COMMENTS: Common throughout Capitol Reef, Arches, Bears Ears, Canyonlands, Grand Staircase, and Glen Canyon.

Synonyms: Physaria didymocarpa var. australis

WATSON'S BLADDERPOD

Physaria intermedia | **Mustard Family** Brassicaceae

An herbaceous perennial that grows as a tiny cushion plant with one to few stems. Foliage is covered with fine, star-shaped hairs. The rootstalk is usually covered with dry, brown leaves remaining from previous years' growth. **Stems** are erect and can reach 6" in height. Basal **leaves** are 3/8" to 2" long, very narrow, entire, and linear. Leaves along the stems are reduced in size. Flowering stalk is usually about ½" long, topped with bright yellow ½" sized **flowers**. **Seedpods** are twice as long as wide, inflated to an ovoid shape, and typically sessile. **Blooms** mid April to August. **Occurs** throughout much of Utah to Arizona and New Mexico. Found in sagebrush, pinyon juniper woodland, ponderosa pine, spruce fir, and bristlecone pine communities. (5,000 to 9,300 feet)

COMMENTS: Found widespread throughout Capitol Reef, although its diminutive size makes it difficult to see. It also occurs in Bryce Canyon and Zion.

PRINCE'S PLUME

Stanleya pinnata | **Mustard Family** Brassicaceae

A large, showy herbaceous perennial typically 2' to 3' tall, but can reach 5' in height. It is a shrubby, vertical-shaped plant. **Stems** are usually simple or with only a few branches. It always appears erect, taller than wide. **Leaves** are 2" to 7" long and 1" to 2" wide, lance shaped to elliptical, with the lower ones being lobed and upper ones entire. Usually few to no hairs on either stems or leaves. Yellow **flowers** grow along the entirety of a tall stalk, blooming first at the lower portion and gradually extending to the tip with blossoms. Flowers are about ½" across. **Seedpods** are long and slender, up to 2½" long and variously erect to spreading or hanging downward along the stalk. **Blooms** May to November. **Occurs** throughout Utah, Idaho to North Dakota, California, Arizona, and New Mexico. Found in mixed desert scrub, sagebrush, and pinyon juniper woodland communities, typically in soils that contain selenium. (2,000 to 9,100 ft)

COMMENTS: Common throughout Capitol Reef. It also occurs in Arches, Canyonlands, Bears Ears, Bryce Canyon, Glen Canyon, Grand Staircase, and Zion. Several American Indian groups use this plant for both food and medicinal purposes. The genus, *Stanleya*, is named after Lord Edward Stanley, who was the president of the Linnaean and Zoological societies in London in the early 1800s.

DESERT PLUME

Stanleya viridiflora | **Mustard Family** Brassicaceae

An herbaceous perennial that reaches 2' to 3' in height, typically in the form of a vertical, shrubby plant. This plant is similar to Prince's Plume in general appearance. **Stems** are usually simple or with only a few branches. It always appears erect, taller than wide. **Leaves** are 2 ¾" to 12" long and ¾" to 3 ½" wide, lance shaped to elliptical, all entire. The lower leaves are usually on a short stalk, while the upper leaves are sessile to the stem. The base of at least the lower leaves is typically heart shaped. Usually there are few to no hairs on either stems or leaves. Yellow **flowers** grow along a tall central stalk. Flowers are about ½" across. **Seedpods** are long and slender, up to 2 ½" long, and variously erect to spreading or declining along the stalk. **Blooms** May to August. **Occurs** scattered throughout Utah, Idaho, Wyoming, Oregon, and Nevada. Found in mixed desert scrub, sagebrush, and pinyon juniper woodland communities usually in the Moenkopi formation or other gypsiferous soils. (2,000 to 9,100 ft)

COMMENTS: Usually seen in the central portion of Capitol Reef.

CANDELABRA THELYPODY

Thelypodiopsis divaricata | **Mustard Family** Brassicaceae

An annual or biennial up to 43" tall, with erect, simple stems. **Stems** are not inflated, but may be covered with long hairs. Basal **leaves** 2/3" to 4" long, up to 1" wide, and irregularly toothed. Leaves on the stems are directly attached to the stem, lance shaped and reduced in size upward. **Flowers** are yellowish with a long claw. They grow along the entirety of the stalk, blooming first at the lower end and gradually extending to the tip with blossoms. **Seedpods** are narrow, up to 1/3" long, and curve upwards. **Blooms** mid April to June. **Occurs** only in south central Utah. Found in mixed desert scrub, shadscale, to pinyon juniper woodlands. Primarily found in seleniferous soils in the Mancos, Dakota, Morrison, Chinle or Moenkopi formations. (4,000 to 6,800 ft)

COMMENTS: This Colorado Plateau endemic is usually seen in the central and southern portions of Capitol Reef, and in Canyonlands and Glen Canyon.

Synonyms: Caulanthus divaricatus

YELLOW BEE PLANT

Peritoma lutea | **Spider Plant Family** Cleomaceae

An annual that grows to 4', but often seen about 18" tall. Flowering **stems** are erect, stout, with only a few branches, and sparingly covered with hairs. **Leaves** have five to seven leaflets that are oblong to lance shaped, ¼" to 2" long and 1/16" to ⅜" wide. Yellow **flowers** grow along an unbranched stalk up to 4" long. **Seeds** form in a pod up to 1¼" long. **Blooms** April to September. **Occurs** throughout Utah to California and New Mexico. Found in salt desert scrub to pinyon juniper and ponderosa pine woodlands on sandy soils, and occasionally in disturbed bottomland soils. (3,900 to 7,900 ft)

COMMENTS: This plant is usually found in the central and northern portions of Capitol Reef. Large fields are especially showy in the North Blue Flats area following good spring rains. It also occurs in Glen Canyon, Arches, Canyonlands, Bears Ears, Bryce Canyon, Grand Staircase, and Zion.

Synonyms: Cleome lutea, Peritoma breviflora

CREEPING RUSH-PEA

Hoffmannseggia repens | **Pea Family** Fabaceae

A perennial herb 3" to 7" tall that may sprawl along the ground or grow erect. **Leaves** are up to 3¾" long, with four to 14 leaflets that are about ½" long and ¼" wide, covered with tiny hairs. **Flower** stalks contain seven to 25 flowers; bright yellow flowers spread outwards at full bloom. Each petal is about ½" long and has a bronze or reddish spot near its base. **Seedpods** hang downwards and are about 2" long, ¾" wide and very hairy. **Blooms** late April to June. **Occurs** in south central Utah and Colorado. Found in sandy soils in mixed desert scrub. (4,700 to 5,500 ft)

COMMENTS: This strikingly beautiful Colorado Plateau endemic can be found most easily along the Highway 95 near Hanksville, Utah. This species most likely occurs in the southern portion of Capitol Reef. It also occurs in Glen Canyon and Grand Staircase.

Synonyms: Caesalpinia repens

YELLOW SWEET CLOVER

Melilotus officinalis | **Pea Family** Fabaceae

An annual that grows up to 5' tall. **Stems** are erect with multiple branches. Compound **leaves** are on short stalks with three wedge shaped leaflets, ¼" to 1½" long. Leaf margins are toothed. Flower stalks have 20 to 65 yellow **flowers** about ¼" long. Flowers fade to cream color when aged. **Seeds** are inconspicuous. **Blooms** May to August. **Occurs** throughout Utah and North America. It typically grows in riparian areas or along roadsides and ditches. (2,800 to 8,000 ft)

COMMENTS: This species was introduced from Europe and has spread throughout North America. It is common in the central and southern portions of Capitol Reef along the Fremont River and in moist canyon bottoms. It also occurs in all Southern Utah parks and monuments.

Synonyms: Medicago officinalis, Melilotus arvensis, Melilotus leucanthus, Melilotus lutea, Melilotus luteus

GOLDEN PEA

Thermopsis montana | **Pea Family** Fabaceae

An herbaceous perennial up to 3' tall with numerous erect stems. **Stems** may be covered with fine hairs. Compound **leaves** have 3 leaflets ¾" to 3½" long, elliptical or lance shaped, usually with tiny soft hairs on the underside. Flower stalks typically are 5" long, with two to 23 flowers. The yellow **flowers** curve upwards at full bloom and are ¾" to 1 1/8" long. **Seedpods** curve upwards, are covered with hairs, and turn black when mature. **Blooms** May to September. **Occurs** throughout Utah, north to British Columbia, south to New Mexico, Arizona, and California. Found in moist spring and seep or riparian areas. (4,100 to 11,200 ft)

COMMENTS: Most commonly found in the northern and central portions of Capitol Reef, and in Bryce Canyon, Cedar Breaks, Grand Staircase, and Zion. Visitors often report seeing this species along the Fremont River Trail in Capitol Reef.

BROOM FLAX

Linum aristatum | **Flax Family** Linaceae

An annual that grows up to 18" tall. **Stems** typically branch from near the base. **Leaves** are linear, narrow, and up to 5/8" long. The yellow to yellow-orange **flowers** are ¾" across, with petals that fall off quickly after maturity. **Seeds** are inconspicuous. **Blooms** April to October. **Occurs** in central and southern Utah, Arizona, New Mexico, and Colorado. Found in sagebrush, mixed desert scrub, pinyon juniper woodland, and ponderosa pine communities. (3,700 to 6,500 ft)

COMMENTS: This delicate wildflower is widespread in canyon bottoms, uplands and benches in the central and southern portions of Capitol Reef, and in Arches, Canyonlands, Bears Ears, Glen Canyon, Grand Staircase, and Zion.

Synonyms: Cathartolinum aristatum, Mesynium aristatum

YELLOW FLAX

Linum puberulum | **Flax Family** Linaceae

An annual that grows up to 8" tall. **Stems** typically branch from near the base and are covered with tiny, fine hairs. **Leaves** are linear, narrow, and up to 5/8" long. The rust orange to salmon **flowers** have darker rust to red coloration near the base and are ¾" to 1" across. **Seeds** are inconspicuous. **Blooms** mid April to July. **Occurs** throughout much of Utah, Arizona, New Mexico, Wyoming, Nebraska, and south to Mexico. Found in mixed desert scrub, saltbush, and pinyon juniper woodland communities. (3,700 to 8,600 ft)

COMMENTS: This delicate wildflower can be seen in canyon bottoms and uplands in the northern and central portions of Capitol Reef, and in Canyonlands and Glen Canyon.

Synonyms: Cathartolinum puberulum, Linum rigidum var. puberulum, Mesynium puberulum

WHITESTEM BLAZING STAR

Mentzelia albicaulis | **Stickleleaf Family** Loasaceae

An annual that grows up to 16" tall with simple or branching stems. **Stems** are white or greenish-white. Foliage is sticky to the touch due to barbed hairs covering the entire plant. Lower **leaves** are lance shaped or linear, up to 6" long, and with entire or lobed margins. Upper leaves are similar but reduced in size. One to three yellow **flowers** about ¾" long occur in a terminal cluster. If multiple flowers are in the cluster, those on the outside may hang downwards. Flowers have five petals. **Seedpods** are cylindrical in shape, covered with barbed hairs and sticky to touch. **Blooms** April to August. **Occurs** throughout Utah, British Columbia to Mexico. Found in sandy soils in mixed desert scrub, sagebrush, saltbush, pinyon juniper woodland, and ponderosa pine communities. (2,800 to 8,000 ft)

COMMENTS: It is widespread throughout Capitol Reef, and in Arches, Canyonlands, Glen Canyon, Grand Staircase, and Zion. The genus, *Mentzelia*, is named after a German botanist Mentzel (1622-1701). Another common name for this genus is "stick leaf," referring to the barbed hairs on foliage. The specific name, *albicaulis*, means "white stemmed."

Synonyms: Acrolasia albicaulis, Acrolasia gracilis, Bartonia albicaulis, Mentzelia gracilis, Mentzelia mojavensis, Trachyphytum gracile

COMMON GLOBEMALLOW

Sphaeralcea coccinea | **Mallow Family** Malvaceae

A perennial up to 18" tall that forms a small bushy shrub. Few to several **stems** arise from a woody base. Foliage is covered with pick shaped gray or yellowish hairs, giving the stems a gray-yellow appearance and the leaves a gray-green color. **Leaves** are deeply lobed, with three to five lobes or teeth per leaf. Leaves are about 1 1/3" long and 2" wide and are usually wider than long giving them an ovate shape. **Flowers** are bright orange, ½" wide, and borne on an elongated stalk or clustered at the stalk tip. **Seedpods** are hard capsules that contain many tiny black seeds. **Blooms** mid April to October. **Occurs** throughout Utah, north to Canada and south to Arizona, New Mexico, and Texas. Found in mixed desert scrub, sagebrush, pinyon juniper woodland, and ponderosa pine communities in wash bottoms and uplands. (3,000 to 9,000 ft)

COMMENTS: Found widespread throughout Capitol Reef. It also occurs in Arches, Canyonlands, Bryce Canyon, Bears Ears, and Zion. Leaf shape of this species differentiates it from the closely related *S. parvifolia*. Navajo Indians have several uses for this species, including healing wounds, stopping bleeding, as a tonic to treat colds and coughs, and as a beverage used in ceremonies. The fruits are reportedly edible. Pollen and seeds have been found in several ruins, suggesting the Ancestral Puebloans used it for food.

Synonyms: Malveopsis coccinea, Sida dissecta

SMALL-LEAF GLOBEMALLOW

Sphaeralcea parvifolia | **Mallow Family** Malvaceae

A perennial up to 24" tall that forms a bushy shrub. Few to several **stems** arise from a woody base. Foliage is covered with gray hairs giving the stems a gray appearance and leaves a gray green color. **Leaves** are oval to kidney shaped and up to 2" long and wide. Leaf margins are slightly lobed and wavy. **Flowers** are orange, up to 1 1/8" across, and borne in a compact cluster often with more than one flower per node. **Seedpods** are hard capsules that contain many tiny black seeds. **Blooms** mid-April to October. **Occurs** throughout much of Utah, Arizona, New Mexico, and California. Found in mixed desert scrub, sagebrush, and pinyon juniper woodlands. Often seen along roadsides. (2,700 to 8,800 ft)

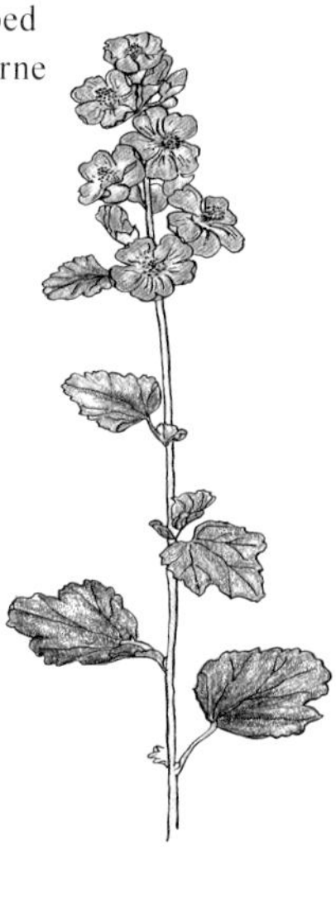

COMMENTS: Found widespread throughout Capitol Reef. It also occurs in Arches, Canyonlands, Bears Ears, Glen Canyon, Bryce Canyon, Grand Staircase, and Zion. Leaf shape of this species differentiates it from the closely related *S. coccinea*. See comments under *S. coccinea* for additional details about the genus.

Synonyms: Sphaeralcea arizonica

LAVENDER OR LAVENDERLEAF SUNDROPS

Calylophus lavandulifolius | **Evening Primrose Family** Onagraceae

A sprawling to erect perennial herb with several **branches** extending 2" to 8" long. Foliage is covered with fine, woolly hairs. **Leaves** are rather small, ¼" to 1¼" long and about ⅛" wide, grayish, and linear to elliptical in shape. They appear to be crowded up along the stems. Large, showy yellow **flowers** bloom from erect buds on solitary stalks. Petals often appear crinkled and the margins are wavy. Flowers fade to reddish orange to lavender with age. **Seeds** are in a capsule ½" to ¾" long. **Blooms** May to August. **Occurs** throughout southern Utah, Nevada, Arizona, Texas, Wyoming, and South Dakota. Found in sandy soils on rocky benches in sagebrush, desert scrub, pinyon juniper, and ponderosa pine woodlands. (4,500 to 9,000 ft)

COMMENTS: Found in the central and southern portions of Capitol Reef, Lavender evening primrose is often found growing in desert scrub or pinyon juniper woodland. It also appears to favor the Summerville Formation in that Park, however, it is not restricted to this Formation. In Bryce Canyon, it is typically found in Ponderosa Pine Woodlands. It also occurs in Canyonlands, Glen Canyon, Grand Staircase, and Bears Ears.

Synonyms: Calylophus hartwegii var. lavandulifolius, Calylophus lavandulifolia, Galpinsia lavandulifolia, Oenothera lavandulifolia

EASTWOOD'S SUNDROPS

Camissonia eastwoodiae | **Evening Primrose Family** Onagraceae

An erect growing annual reaching 2" to 40" tall. These plants are typically single **stemmed**. Foliage tends to be smooth. **Leaves** are typically restricted to the lower portion of the stem, are simple or irregularly toothed, and up to 2 1/3" long and ¼" to 1½" wide. Numerous bright yellow **flowers** spotted with red dots grow along in a nodding elongated flower stalk. Flowers are ½" to 5/8" across and fade to cream as they dry. **Seed** capsules are curved (up to 1½" long) and cylindrical in shape. **Blooms** mid-April to June. **Occurs** in southern Utah to Arizona, and Colorado; it is a Colorado Plateau endemic. Found in clay to sandy soils of uplands, hills, or canyons in sagebrush, mixed desert scrub, and juniper woodland communities. (3,900 to 5,900 ft)

COMMENTS: Usually seen in the southern portion of Capitol Reef. It also occurs in Glen Canyon, Grand Staircase, and Arches.

Synonyms: Oenothera eastwoodiae, Oenothera scapoidea var. eastwoodiae

HOOKER'S EVENING PRIMROSE

Oenothera elata | **Evening Primrose Family** Onagraceae

A biennial herb that can grow to heights of 5' tall. **Stems** are primarily simple and unbranched. Foliage is covered with glands and short, stiff hairs. A close look reveals long hairs scattered amongst the shorter hairs along the stem. **Leaves** grow along the stem (rather than basally), generally have toothed margins, and vary from long and slender to elliptical in shape. Lower leaves are on a short stalk, while upper leaves are generally sessile. Leaves reduce in both length and width as they ascend the stem, and are ¾" to 12" long and ⅛" to 1⅜" wide. Yellow **flowers** are large and showy, fading reddish orange with age. The fused portion of the calyx and corolla below the petals is between 1" to 2" long. (This is a key distinguishing feature of this species.) **Seed** capsules are ¾" to 1¾" long and very narrow. **Blooms** May to November. **Occurs** throughout Utah, from Washington, Montana, California, and Arizona to Central America. It is restricted to moist areas such as riparian areas, springs, or seeps in sagebrush, mixed desert scrub, mixed conifer woodlands, aspen, and spruce fir communities. (4,500 to 9,100 ft)

COMMENTS: Found infrequently in canyon bottoms in the central and southern portions of Capitol Reef. It also occurs in Glen Canyon and Bears Ears. This species was previously known as *Oenothera hookeri*, named for Sir Joseph Dalton Hooker (1817-1911), an English botanist and director of the Royal Botanic Garden at Kew in 1865.

BRONZE EVENING PRIMROSE

Oenothera howardii | **Evening Primrose Family** Onagraceae

A low growing, perennial herb with no **stems**. All **leaves** are basal, can be up to 8" long, and usually about 1" wide. They are on stalks and have entire or irregularly toothed margins. Large and brilliant yellow **flowers** begin fading to bronze or maroon by midday. They grow on single stalks that sprout from the base of the plant. **Seed** capsules are nearly round, 1¼" long and ½" to ¾" wide. **Blooms** May to July. **Occurs** throughout most of Utah to Nevada, Colorado, and Kansas. Found in rocky or clay soils on hills or benches in mixed desert scrub, pinyon juniper woodland, and ponderosa pine woodlands. (4,500 to 9,300 ft)

COMMENTS: Found in the central and southern portions of Capitol Reef. It is often seen growing in Moenkopi or Chinle formations, however it is not restricted to these formations and may be found on others. Around Bryce Canyon, it is often seen growing on limestone soils. It also occurs in Canyonlands, Grand Staircase, and Zion.

Synonyms: Lavauxia howardii

FREMONT'S BUCKWHEAT

Eriogonum corymbosum var. aureum | **Buckwheat Family** Polygonaceae

A fairly large clump forming shrub that reaches up to 4' tall and is just about as wide. In our area, it is usually about 18" to 24" tall. This is a complex and highly variable species. **Leaves** are lance shaped, elliptical, oval, or rounded, and ¼" to 1½"long. Leaves may be densely covered with fine woolly hairs or smooth and free of hairs on one or both sides. The tiny white or yellow **flowers** grow in flat topped, terminal clusters on naked flower stalks. Flowers lack petals but have petal like sepals. **Seeds** are inconspicuous. **Blooms** August to November. **Occurs** throughout much of Utah, to Arizona, and Colorado. Found on sandy to clay soils in mixed desert scrub, sagebrush, blackbrush, pinyon juniper woodland, up to ponderosa pine communities. (3,000 to 9,000 ft)

COMMENTS: Some species of *Eriogonum* hybridize, which can make identification to the species or varietal level a challenge. This variety is common throughout the Capitol Reef, particularly along the scenic drive and in Fruita. This variety of buckwheat also occurs in Zion and Glen Canyon. The specific name, *corymbosum*, refers to the flat-topped inflorescence.

Synonyms: Eriogonum aureum, Eriogonum effusum subsp. nelsonil, Eriogonum microthecum subsp. aureum, Eriogonum microthecum var. crispum

SAND BUCKWHEAT

Eriogonum leptocladon | **Buckwheat Family** Polygonaceae

A fairly large clump-forming shrub that reaches up to 30" tall. Plants have slender **stems**. **Leaves** are linear, ⅜" to 1¾" long and are usually covered with fine woolly hairs on one or both sides. The tiny yellow to whitish **flowers** may be tinted with pink and they grow in flat or rounded topped, terminal clusters. Flowers lack petals but have petal like sepals. **Seeds** are inconspicuous. **Blooms** August to November. **Occurs** in southern Utah, to Arizona, New Mexico, and Colorado. Found on sandy soils in saltbush, sand sagebrush, blackbrush, and juniper woodland communities. (4,300 to 6,200 ft)

COMMENTS: There is a yellow flowered variety (*Eriogonum leptocladon var. leptocladon*) and a white flowered (tinged with pink) variety (*Eriogonum leptocladon var. ramosissimum*) that otherwise look similar. The white flowered variety is widespread throughout Capitol Reef; the yellow flowered variety is most commonly seen in the Cathedral Valley area of Capitol Reef. Both varieties occur in Glen Canyon, Arches, and Canyonlands.

SULFUR BUCKWHEAT

Eriogonum umbellatum | **Buckwheat Family** Polygonaceae

A small perennial mat-forming plant with woody branches. The woody base is covered with persistent leaf bases and dried leaves. **Leaves** are oval to elliptic, about 1 1/8" long and ¾" wide. They may be densely covered with fine woolly hairs or smooth and free of hairs. The tiny yellow or cream-colored **flowers** grow in flat topped, terminal clusters on naked flower stalks. Individual flowers are bell shaped and may be suffused with red. **Seeds** are inconspicuous. **Blooms** August to October. **Occurs** throughout Utah, to Arizona, Nevada, California, Colorado, Montana, and north to Canada. Found in mixed desert scrub, sagebrush, pinyon juniper woodland, up to spruce fir communities. (4,500 to 12,200 ft)

COMMENTS: It is most often seen in the central portion of Capitol Reef. It also occurs in all the Southern Utah parks. There are several highly variable varieties of this species and it has been found to hybridize with other species of buckwheat. It is a showy plant when in full bloom. Many species within this genus contain saponin, a slightly toxic chemical that may lead to a severe stomachache if eaten. Along the same lines, several American Indian cultures used a liquid concentrate made from buckwheat rootstalks as an emetic for treating stomachaches. Other medicinal uses attributed to American Indians include an earache remedy, infection prevention, and eyewash. Plants in this genus were reportedly an important food source in prehistoric times.

BLACKBRUSH

Coleogyne ramosissima | **Rose Family** Rosaceae

A long-lived perennial shrub that reaches 6' in height, but is typically seen 2' to 3' tall. This rounded shrub has numerous, intricate branches; branch ends are spine tipped. Old bark is grayish and peels off easily. **Leaves** grow in tight clusters from single fascicles; they are covered with tiny, anvil shaped hairs that are attached to the leaf surface near the middle of the hair rather than at one end. (¼" to ½" long). Bright yellow **flowers** are solitary on branch ends. Petals are rarely seen on this shrub; the sepals, which are arranged in two rows, are what you notice (¼" to 1/3" long). Yellow stamens are numerous (20 to 40 per flower). **Seeds** are inconspicuous. **Blooms** May to June. **Occurs** from southern California through southern Nevada, Arizona, southern Utah to southwestern Colorado. Found in sandy to clay soils in upland desert scrub and pinyon-juniper woodlands. (3,700 to 6,260 ft)

COMMENTS: It is found in the southern portions of Capitol Reef, and in Arches, Canyonlands, Bears Ears, Zion, and Glen Canyon. This species can be the dominant shrub over large expanses of landscape. In Utah, it often occurs in mixed stands with Mormon Tea (*Ephedra* spp.). Blackbrush is not palatable to livestock or wild horses, but is eaten by bighorn sheep and deer. The common name comes from that fact that after rainstorms when the bark is wet, the plant appears black.

BITTERBRUSH

Purshia tridentata | **Rose Family** Rosaceae

A sprawling, evergreen shrub that reaches 5' in height, with numerous intricate **branches**. Plants are more typically seen 2' to 3' tall and tend to large dense mats. They are fragrant when in bloom. **Leaves** grow in clusters along the branch, are wedge shaped, and primarily three toothed. Leaves are thick and leathery with the upper surface a dark green and the underside white woolly. Showy yellow **flowers** have five petals and are ½" to 1" across. **Seeds** are up to ¾" long and oval, narrowing to a slender tip. **Blooms** April to July. **Occurs** throughout Utah, the western United States, and north to Canada. Found on dry slopes in mixed desert scrub, sagebrush, pinyon juniper woodland, and ponderosa pine communities. (4,000 to 9,100 ft)

COMMENTS: It is common in the northern portion of Capitol Reef, and also found in Arches, Bryce Canyon, Cedar Breaks, Canyonlands, and Zion. American Indians reportedly used this plant medicinally to treat eye infections and as a cough medicine. This plant is favored forage for several species of wildlife.

BLUE, LAVENDER TO PURPLE FLOWERS

DESERT STAR JASMINE

Amsonia tomentosa | **Dogbane Family** Apocynaceae

A medium sized, dense shrub, 8" to 24" tall. **Leaves** are linear to lance shaped. They may be covered with dense woolly hairs and grayish green, or smooth and bright green. Showy bluish-white **flowers** grow in terminal clusters; they are ⅜" to ¾" long with slender tube-shaped petals that flare broadly at the top. Brown **seed** capsules are cup shaped, 1½" to 2½" long and ½" to 1" broad, with a smooth outer surface. **Blooms** April to June. **Occurs** in southern Utah, New Mexico, Arizona, and south to Mexico. Commonly found in sandy soils, often in canyon bottoms, in desert scrub, grassland, or blackbrush communities. (3,200 to 5,200 ft)

COMMENTS: Found only in the very southern portions of Capitol Reef. It also occurs in Arches, Canyonlands, Bears Ears, and Glen Canyon. The specific name, *tomentosa*, refers to densely matted woolly hairs on leaves and stems of some plants.

UTAH DAISY

Erigeron utahensis | **Sunflower Family** Asteraceae

An herbaceous perennial up to 2' tall. **Stems** and leaves are covered with stiff, gray to whitish hairs that give the plant a grayish appearance. **Leaves** are ½" to 4" long and very narrow and linear. Leaves are entire with the upper ones being much reduced. **Flower heads** are solitary or in clusters. Ray flowers are white to pink or purple, about ½" across. Disk flowers are a bright yellow cluster. This is a showy plant when in full bloom. Tiny **seeds** are linear with twin rows of bristles. **Blooms** mid April to July. **Occurs** in central and southern Utah, Colorado, and Arizona. It typically grows in sandy soils in desert scrub, blackbrush, and pinyon juniper communities. (4,000 to 8,000 ft)

COMMENTS: Flower cup size differentiates one variety that is widespread in the central and southern portions of Capitol Reef from a second variety that is rarely seen in the very southern tip of Capitol Reef. This species also occurs in Arches, Canyonlands, Bears Ears, Glen Canyon, Grand Staircase, and Zion.

Synonyms: Erigeron utahensis var sparsifolius, and Erigeron utahensis var. utahensis

CONSTANCE'S PHACELIA

Phacelia constancei | **Borage Family** Boraginaceae

An erect biennial that grows 6" to 16" tall. **Stems** are thick, covered with fine hairs and glands, and may be reddish in mature plants. **Leaves** have wavy or toothed margins; the basal leaves grow on a short stalk. Leaves growing along the stem become sessile; they are covered with glandular hairs. Bell shaped, purple to lavender **flowers** grow in a strong curving "scorpion tail" shape at stem ends. **Seed** pods are globe shaped with four small seeds in each pod. **Blooms** June to September. **Occurs** in Colorado, northern Arizona, and southeastern Utah. Found in sandy soils in salt desert scrub and juniper woodlands. (4,100 to 6,600 ft)

COMMENTS: This is an uncommon Colorado Plateau endemic that is occasionally seen in Bears Ears. It has not been recorded in Capitol Reef to date.

NOTCH LEAVED SCORPIONWEED

Phacelia crenulata | **Borage Family** Boraginaceae

A biennial that sprouts a basal rosette of leaves in the first year and blooms and sets seed in the second year. It is an ill-scented plant; foliage is covered with stiff, glandular hairs. Flowering **stems** are erect, 3" to 32" tall. Stems are stout, olive green in color. Basal **leaves** grow on a short stalk, are deeply lobed and up to 3" long. Leaves on the stem become sessile and reduced in size upward. **Flowers** grow in a terminal spike that curls strongly like a scorpion's tail. They are small (about ¼" across), tubular, and blue violet to purple. Corolla lobes are bell shaped. Stamens and style extend beyond the corolla lobes. Style is forked for about half its length. **Seeds** are inconspicuous. **Blooms** mid April to June. **Occurs** in central and southern Utah, Nevada, New Mexico, Colorado, and Arizona. Found in salt desert scrub and pinyon juniper woodlands. (3,500 to 8,500 ft)

COMMENTS: Commonly seen in the central and southern portions of Capitol Reef. It also occurs in Arches, Bryce Canyon, Bears Ears, Canyonlands, Grand Staircase, and Glen Canyon. Glandular hairs on leaves and stems can cause a rash similar to that of poison ivy. Some species of *Phacelia* were historically used by Ancestral Puebloans to treat rashes, swellings, and sprains. They used the powdered root or leaves mixed with water. This genus has been reported as an indicator of prehistoric cultivated fields in the southwestern U.S. The common name for this genus, scorpion weed, is indicative of the flower stalk, which often curls at the end like a scorpion's tail.

BRITTLE SCORPIONWEED

Phacelia demissa | **Borage Famil**y Boraginaceae

A low growing annual with numerous succulent, prostrate to upright branches. This plant is usually wider than it is tall. In good years, plants may reach 8" tall, but are typically seen closer to 4" to 5" in height. **Stems** are reddish and brittle when green and fresh. The entire plant is covered with stiff, glandular hairs. **Leaves** grow on a short stalk, are oval, with entire to slightly wavy margins. **Flowers** in open terminal spikes that slightly curl like a scorpion's tail. They are small (about ¼" across), lavender to purple with yellow corolla tubes. Corolla lobes tend to be bell shaped. Stamens and style do not extend beyond the corolla lobes. **Seeds** are inconspicuous. **Blooms** May to June. **Occurs** in central and southern Utah, Wyoming, New Mexico, Colorado, and Arizona. Found on barren clay slopes in saltbush scrub to pinyon juniper woodlands, typically in Dakota, Morrison, Mancos Shale, and Chinle formations. (4,300 to 7,200 ft)

COMMENTS: Commonly seen in southern portions of Capitol Reef. Following extensive fall and winter precipitation, large showy fields of this species are often seen in North Blue Flats and along Highway 24 near Caineville. It also occurs in Arches, Bryce Canyon, Grand Staircase, and Glen Canyon.

SAN RAFAEL PHACELIA

Phacelia rafaelensis | **Borage Family** Boraginaceae

A biennial that in the first year sprouts a basal rosette of leaves and in the second year blooms and sets seed. It has a slightly sweet odor. Flowering **stems** are erect, 5" to 20" tall, but typically about 10" tall. Stems are stout, brownish to olive green in color and covered with glandular hairs. Basal **leaves** grow on a short stalk, have a wavy, toothed margin, and are ¾" to 2¾" long and ⅛" to ⅝" wide. Leaves on the stem are sessile and smaller than the basal leaves. All leaves are covered with glandular, stiff hairs. **Flowers** grow in a terminal cluster with the lower flowers maturing first. Flowers are small (about ¼" across), tubular (tube is grooved) and pale lavender. Corolla lobes spread outward from the tube. Stamens and style extend beyond the corolla lobes by about ⅛". Style is forked for about three-fourths of its length. One of the key features to identifying this *Phacelia* is that the **seeds** are concave on the underside surface and greater than ⅛" in length. **Blooms** April to June. **Occurs** in southern Utah and Arizona. Found in salt desert scrub and pinyon juniper woodlands, primarily in Moenkopi, Carmel, Chinle, or Summerville formations. (3,500 to 6,000 ft)

COMMENTS: It is a Colorado Plateau endemic and a National Park Service sensitive species. Type locality is at Fruita in Capitol Reef National Park. It also occurs in Zion and Glen Canyon.

WESTERN SPIDERWORT

Tradescantia occidentalis | **Spiderwort Family** Commelinaceae

An herbaceous perennial standing 8" to 16" tall. **Leaves** are smooth, green and erect. They have a similar growth form to iris leaves. Large, beautiful purple to magenta colored, three-petaled **flowers** grow in a terminal cluster on the main stem, with two or three leafy bracts below the cluster. Oblong **seed** capsules are about ¼" long, filled with tiny seeds. **Blooms** mid April to August. **Occurs** in southern Utah, Arizona to Texas and North Dakota. Typically found in fine textured sandy soils in sagebrush, pinyon juniper, ponderosa pine, or grassland communities. (4,000 to 7,000 ft)

COMMENTS: This beautiful wildflower occurs in sandy soils primarily in the southern portions of Capitol Reef. It also occurs in Glen Canyon, Grand Staircase, and Zion. These wildflowers got their common name, Spiderwort, either from the fact that the milky sap from broken stems forms web-like filaments when exposed to air or because the angular leaf arrangement resembles a sitting spider. The sap of the plant is said to irritate the skin and cause redness. The genus name comes from John Tradescant, who came to North America to collect plants in the mid 1600s. His father was the royal gardener to King Charles I, and Tradescant took over this position upon his father's death.

Synonyms: Tradescantia virginiana var. occidentalis

BICKNELL MILKVETCH

Astragalus consobrinus | **Pea Family** Fabaceae

A perennial herb that grows from a basal stock, with no above ground branching stems. Plant is only about 2" tall with an overall appearance of a small, silvery gray clump. Typically, there are no **stems**. Roots are covered with persistent, distinct leaf-like appendages (not joined to adjacent ones) up to ¼" long and densely hairy on the outward surface. Each compound **leaf** is up to 2" long with three to eleven leaflets that are ¼" long and less than ⅛" wide. Leaflets are rounded to pointed and hairy on both sides. Foliage is covered with fine hairs. The flowering stem is about 1¼" tall; each flower stalk has two to ten **flowers**. The tiny, ½" long flowers are cream colored tinged with purple, sessile and grow curving upwards on the stalk. **Seedpods** also curve upwards, are sessile, oval (up to ¾" long, to ¼" wide), and covered with stiff, straight hairs. One of the key features to identifying this milkvetch is that the seedpods are laterally compressed only near the tip. **Blooms** April to July. **Occurs** only in south central Utah. Found from sagebrush, mixed desert scrub to pinyon juniper woodlands on Mancos Shale, volcanic gravels, or barren gravelly or sandy hillsides. (5,200 to 9,000 ft)

COMMENTS: This species closely resembles *A. laccoliticus* in growth form and overall coloration, however *A. laccoliticus* has much larger flowers and fruit. This is a Colorado Plateau endemic and National Park Service sensitive species. It is found throughout Capitol Reef.

RIMROCK MILKVETCH

Astragalus desperatus | **Pea Family** Fabaceae

A perennial herb from 1" to 4" in height that grows from short branching stems. Overall appearance is of a small, silvery gray tuft with tiny pink purple flowers. Foliage is covered with fine hairs. Branch nodes are often hidden by leaf like appendages; these appendages may be fused together and sheath the nodes. They are 1/16" to ⅜" long. Compound **leaves** are between ⅜" to 4¾" long with seven to seventeen leaflets. Leaflets are 1/16" to ½" long and less than ⅛" wide, oval to pointed, and hairy either on both sides or only on the underside. Flowering stalk is ¼" to 4" tall, with each inflorescence having only three to eighteen **flowers**. The tiny, ¼" wide flowers are pink purple, pink and white, or purple and white, and may either curve up or down at full bloom. **Seedpods** hang downward and are straight or nearly so; they may be sessile or grow on a short stalk, and typically are lance to oval in shape. They are 1/16" to ⅜" long, covered with long, straight hairs, and have a single seed chamber. **Blooms** May to July. **Occurs** only in the Colorado Plateau region in southern Utah, Arizona, and Colorado. Found on sandstone ledges or the sandy basins among sandstone domes and is associated with pinyon juniper woodlands and mixed desert scrub communities. (4,690 to 7,000 ft)

COMMENTS: More than one variety occurs in Capitol Reef. One of them is a National Park Service sensitive variety, *Astragalus desperatus var. petrophilus* (the variety name means "rock-loving.") This species also occurs in Arches, Bryce Canyon, Canyonlands, and Glen Canyon.

CAINEVILLE MILKVETCH

Astragalus laccoliticus | **Pea Family** Fabaceae

An herbaceous perennial that sprawls along the ground. **Stems** are prostrate (if present) and reach 2⅓" in length. **Leaves** are ¾" to 4" long with five to seventeen leaflets ⅛" to ⅔" long and 1/16" to ⅓" wide. Leaflets are oval to lance shaped with the narrow end near the base and hairy on both sides. **Flower stalks** are ⅔" to 3" tall, containing two to eleven flowers each. The rather large flowers are cream, tinged with purple, and are spreading to ascending at full bloom. **Seedpods** are ¾" to 12/3" long, ascending and sessile. They are typically oval in shape with the tip being laterally compressed. (The pod gives the impression of a boat with an up curved prow.) Pods are not mottled, but are green to purplish, and have thick fleshy interior segments. **Blooms** April to May. **Occurs** only in south central Utah. Found in mixed desert scrub communities typically in Mancos shale formation. (4,700 to 6,000 ft)

COMMENTS: This endemic is a National Park Service sensitive species. It is found in the southern portions of Capitol Reef.

SANDSTONE MILKVETCH

Astragalus sesquiflorus | **Pea Family** Fabaceae

A mat-forming perennial herb that grows prostrate along the ground. Foliage is covered with fine hairs, giving the plant a faint grayish green tint. Compound **leaves** are between ⅜" to 1½" long with seven to 13 leaflets up to ⅜" long and less than 1⁄16" wide. Leaflets are elliptic or egg shaped and hairy on both sides. **Flower** stalk is up to 2" long, with each stalk having one to four flowers. The tiny, ⅜" wide flowers are pink purple and may either curve up or spread outwards at full bloom. **Seedpods** are declining and straight or nearly so, sessile, and typically are oblong in shape. They are 1⁄16" to ⅜" long, covered with long hairs and are compressed in a three-angled shape. **Blooms** May to August. **Occurs** only in southern Utah, Arizona, and Colorado. It is typically found in mixed desert scrub, pinyon juniper, and ponderosa pine woodlands. Found in silty clay and sandy soils, usually associated with rocky ledges or the sandy canyon bottoms in sandstone formations. (3,600 to 10,000 ft)

COMMENTS: Most commonly found in canyon bottoms in the central portion of Capitol Reef, and in Canyonlands, Grand Staircase, and Glen Canyon.

SILVERY LUPINE

Lupinus argenteus | **Pea Family** Fabaceae

A large perennial that grows as an herbaceous shrub up to 2½' tall. Foliage is covered with fine, stiff hairs. Compound **leaves** are palmately divided, ½" to 3" long, with six to nine spatula to linear shaped leaflets. Leaflets are 2¾" to 3¾" long and may be flat or folded lengthwise. Floral spikes have 15 to 92 bluish purple flowers. **Flowers** are about ½" long; the upper petal has a white or yellowish central spot. **Seedpods** are about ¾" long, and may be covered with fine, woolly hairs. **Blooms** mid April to August. **Occurs** throughout Utah and the western United States. Found in mixed desert scrub, sagebrush, pinyon juniper woodland, and spruce fir communities. (4,700 to 5,000 ft)

COMMENTS: This is a highly variable species throughout its range. Two separate varieties are known to occur in Capitol Reef and are occasionally seen in the northern and central portions of that Park. It occurs in all the Southern Utah parks and monuments. Ancient Egyptians cultivated plants in this genus as food and it is still used for this purpose in the Mediterranean. The beans are ground for use in food dishes and are high in protein. Some species of lupine contain alkaloids that are poisonous to livestock, particularly sheep. This is a complex genus with over 600 species worldwide.

DWARF LUPINE

Lupinus pusillus | **Pea Family** Fabaceae

A small annual that grows up to 9" tall. Foliage is covered with soft, spreading hairs. Compound **leaves** are palmately divided, up to 3½" long, with three to nine spatula to linear shaped leaflets. Leaflets are ½" to 1½" long and may be flat or folded lengthwise. Floral spikes have four to 38 blue flowers. **Flowers** are about ½" long; the upper petal has a yellow or white central spot. **Seedpods** contain two seeds; pods are oval in shape with a constriction between the two seeds. **Blooms** April to July. **Occurs** throughout Utah and the western United States. Found in mixed desert scrub, sagebrush, pinyon juniper woodland, and spruce fir communities. (2,500 to 6,500 ft)

COMMENTS: Common throughout Capitol Reef. It also occurs in Arches, Canyonlands, Bears Ears, Glen Canyon, Grand Staircase, and Zion. See comments under *L. argenteus* for more about this genus.

MOUNTAIN LOCOWEED

Oxytropis oreophila var. juniperiana | **Pea Family** Fabaceae

A small, densely tufted herbaceous perennial without **stems** but with silvery, green leaves. Plants appear as tiny clumps or mounds on the ground reaching only 2" to 3" tall. Compound **leaves** are basal, ⅛" to ¾" long, with seven to eleven leaflets. Leaflets are oblong to elliptical and covered with dense, silvery hairs. **Flower** stalks have two to twelve flowers. The tiny (less than ½" long) pink to pink-purple flowers tend to curve upwards at full bloom. Floral bracts are woolly with hairs. Oval **seedpods** curve up at maturity, are sessile, and are covered with hairs. **Blooms** June to August. **Occurs** in south central Utah and Nevada. Found in pinyon juniper, sagebrush, ponderosa pine, and bristlecone pine communities. (6,300 to 9,500 ft)

COMMENTS: Found in the higher elevations of the northern portion of Capitol Reef and on Miners Mountain in that Park. It also occurs in Bryce Canyon.

DUNE SCURFPEA

Psoralidium lanceolatum | **Pea Family** Fabaceae

An herbaceous perennial forming a delicate, open rounded clump up to 16" tall. Compound **leaves** are up to 2" long, with three leaflets. Leaflets are ½" to 2" long and ⅓" wide, lance shaped, but attached at the narrow end. Leaves may be covered with fine hairs on one or both surfaces, or be smooth without hairs, but are always covered with oily glands. Floral spikes are up to 9" long, with five to 41 flowers per spike. **Flowers** are bi-colored white with blue purple, ¼" long with a bell shaped corolla tube. **Seedpods** are densely glandular. **Blooms** April to September. **Occurs** in central and southern Utah, Oklahoma, California, Washington, Canada, Arizona, and New Mexico. Found in sandy soils in mixed desert scrub and pinyon juniper woodlands. (4,000 to 5,800 ft)

COMMENTS: Common in central and southern portions of Capitol Reef. It also occurs in Arches, Canyonlands, Bears Ears, Glen Canyon, Grand Staircase, and Zion. American Indians from the Great Plains region used the oily, aromatic leaves of this species as a moisturizer. Other parts of the plant were also used to treat headaches and to clear up hoarseness in the throat.

Synonyms: Psoralea lanceolata, Psoralea micrantha, Psoralea scabra, Psoralea stenostachys

THOMPSON'S INDIGO BUSH

Psorothamnus thompsoniae | **Pea Family** Fabaceae

A large, sprawling shrub that reaches 3' in height and has numerous spiny branches. New **branches** are velvety with short, backwards curving hairs and are conspicuously dotted with yellow or orange, odorous glands. Compound **leaves** are ¼" to 2" long with seven to seventeen leaflets. The tiny leaflets are no longer than ⅓" (usually shorter) and are linear to oval. Leaves may be glandular or hairy or smooth. Flowers grow on elongated stalks no longer than 4", containing eight to 25 flowers. Purple pink or indigo **flowers** are about ½" in length. Calyx lobes are oval in shape. **Seedpods** are covered with tiny glands. **Blooms** May to July. **Occurs** in south central Utah. Found in mixed desert scrub, blackbrush, pinyon juniper, and desert grassland communities. (3,700 to 7,500 ft)

COMMENTS: This is a Colorado Plateau endemic. This species occurs just east of Capitol Reef, and in Canyonlands, Bears Ears, and Glen Canyon. A closely related and very similar species, *Psorothamnus fremontii*, occurs in the southern portion of Capitol Reef. These two species look very much alike, differing primarily in that *P. fremontii* does not have the yellow orange glands on the new stem growth.

Synonyms: Parosela thompsoniae

FRINGE-LEAF NECKLACEPOD

Sophora stenophylla | **Pea Family** Fabaceae

A long-lived herbaceous perennial that reaches 5" to 16" tall. It grows from long underground spreading rootstalks. **Leaves** are linear and narrow, with a feathery appearance. They are covered with silvery hairs. Blue, scented **flowers** (½" to 1" long) grow along unbranched stems on short stalks. There can be ten to thirty flowers along each stalk. **Seed** pods are spreading to slightly declining about 2" long and ⅓" wide. They tend to be hairy and contain one to five seeds. **Blooms** April to May. **Occurs** in Arizona, New Mexico and southern Utah. Found in sand dunes or other sandy soil areas in desert scrub, blackbrush, sagebrush, pinyon juniper woodlands, to ponderosa pine forests. (4,500 to 6,300 ft)

COMMENTS: This is a Colorado Plateau endemic that is occasionally seen in Bears Ears, Arches, Canyonlands, and Glen Canyon. It has not been recorded in Capitol Reef to date. Foliage and seeds contain an alkaloid that can be toxic to livestock or humans if large amounts are ingested.

Synonyms: Vexibia stenophylla

WINDING MARIPOSA LILY

Calochortus flexuosus | **Lily Family** (Liliaceae)

This lily has a twining or zigzagging stem so the plant appears to be winding along the ground. **Stems** are branching, between 7" and 16" long. It grows from an underground bulb. The few, scraggly **leaves** are linear and slightly curled. Tulip shaped **flowers** are 1" to 1½" across and pale lavender in color. Sepals are similarly colored. Each petal has a yellow band and a purple dot located around its inner base. **Seeds** are three angled capsules 1" to 2" long. **Blooms** April to June. **Occurs** from southern California east through Arizona, and southern Utah to northwestern New Mexico and southwestern Colorado. Typically grows in dry rocky soils on mesas or dry slopes in blackbrush, shadscale, sagebrush, to pinyon-juniper woodlands. (3,900 to 5,800 feet)

COMMENTS: This species has not been recorded in Capitol Reef, however it does occur in Canyonlands, Bears Ears, Zion and Glen Canyon. After wet winters, large fields of these lilies can be seen along Highway 95 between Hite and Fry Canyon.

BLUE FLAX

Linum perenne | **Flax Family** Linaceae

A perennial herb that grows up to 30" tall. **Stems** are typically unbranching and have numerous leaves extending their entire length. Basal **leaves** are very narrow and up to 1¼" long. Leaves on the stem are also linear, narrow, and shorter than the basal leaves. The blue **flowers** are up to 1" across and grow in terminal clusters. Flowers may have a whitish or yellowish base. Petals quickly fall off after flowers reach maturity. **Seeds** resemble a small tan globe. **Blooms** April to August. **Occurs** throughout Utah, north to Alaska and south to Mexico. Found in sagebrush, mixed desert scrub, pinyon juniper woodland, and spruce fir communities. (4,000 to 11,600 ft)

COMMENTS: This pretty wildflower is seen in canyon bottoms, uplands, and benches throughout Capitol Reef, and in all the Southern Utah parks. A similar looking European species, *Linum usitatissimum,* is often sold as a native wildflower. Both the native and the cultivated flax have been introduced to many locations in the West through reclamation plantings. American Indians had several medicinal uses for blue flax including eyewash, a tonic, and for treating wounds.

DWARF LOUSEWORT

Pedicularis centranthera **Broomrape Family** Orobanchaceae

A ground hugging perennial that reaches only about 3" tall. Deep green **leaves** (2" to 9" long and up to 1" wide) are deeply toothed, occasionally appearing to have double dentation. They grow in a basal rosette around the short stem that sprouts from a tuberous rootstalk. **Flowers** grow in dense clusters at the top of each stem near the central portion of the plant. Individual flowers are ¾" to 1⅓" long and are dark lavender with the upper lip sometimes white or yellowish in color. **Seeds** are inconspicuous. **Blooms** March to May. **Occurs** in Oregon, Nevada, Wyoming, Arizona, and Utah. Found in pinyon-juniper, ponderosa pine, Douglas Fir, aspen, white pine to spruce forests. (5,000 to 10,400 ft)

COMMENTS: It occasionally occurs in the central portion of Capitol Reef primarily in pinyon-juniper woodlands. It also occurs in Bears Ears, Canyonlands, Bryce Canyon, Glen Canyon, and Zion. The genera *Pedicularis* comes from the Latin *pediculus,* which means "louse." Shoshone people use portions of this plant to treat stomachaches.

NARROWLEAF PENSTEMON

Penstemon angustifolius | **Plantago Family** Plantaginaceae

A perennial herb up to 24" tall with few to many erect **stems**. The foliage and stems are green in color. **Leaves** are ¾" to 3¾" long, narrow, lance shaped and leathery to touch. Upper leaves are clasping, inversely lance shaped and wider from the middle upwards along the stem. Lavender to pale blue, tubular **flowers** grow in an elongated spike. Each flower is moderately inflated and ¾" to 1" long. They extend outward when in full bloom. **Seeds** are inconspicuous. **Blooms** mid April to June. **Occurs** in central and southern Utah, Colorado, Arizona, and New Mexico. Found in canyons, on hills or benches in mixed desert scrub, saltbush, sagebrush, and pinyon juniper woodlands. (3,900 to 7,200 ft)

COMMENTS: Occasionally seen in the southern portion of Capitol Reef, most commonly reported by visitors along the Burr Trail. It also occurs in Glen Canyon and Grand Staircase.

MAT PENSTEMON

Penstemon caespitosus | **Plantago Family** Plantaginaceae

A tiny, densely tufted, mat forming perennial with sprawling **stems** up to 5½" long. Plant is rarely more than 2" tall. Foliage and stems are covered with flattened hairs making the plant grayish green in color. **Leaves** are ⅛" to 2/3" long and up to ¼" wide, linear to oval or spatula shaped. One to three lavender pink **flowers** grow at the end of flowering stems. Each flower is about ½" long. **Seeds** are inconspicuous. **Blooms** late May to July. **Occurs** in southern and central Utah and Arizona. Found in sandy soils on rocky uplands in pinyon juniper, sagebrush, and ponderosa pine communities. (6,500 to 9,200 ft)

COMMENTS: Found in the central portion of Capitol Reef, most commonly on Miners Mountain. It also occurs in Bryce Canyon and Cedar Breaks.

FLESHY PENSTEMON

Penstemon carnosus | **Plantago Family** Plantaginaceae

A perennial herb up to 24" tall with few to many erect stems. Foliage and **stems** are often grayish green in color. **Leaves** are thick and fleshy, ¾" to 3½" long and up to 1¼" wide. Most leaves are basal, these being on a short stalk and spatula shaped or oval. Leaves on the stems are clasping and smaller in size. Lavender pink to blue violet **flowers** grow in a congested spike. Each flower is about ¾" long. **Seeds** are inconspicuous. **Blooms** mid April to July. **Occurs** only in central and southern Utah. Found in sandy soils on rocky uplands, hills, or benches in saltbush, sagebrush, or pinyon juniper woodlands. (5,000 to 8,500 ft)

COMMENTS: This Colorado Plateau endemic can be found in the central and southern portions of Capitol Reef, and in Glen Canyon. Plants from Wayne County may show characters of several other closely related *Penstemons*, making proper identification of this plant challenging.

DUSTY PENSTEMON

Penstemon comarrhenus | **Plantago Family** Plantaginaceae

A perennial herb up to 4' tall with few erect stems. Foliage and **stems** are often grayish green in color. Basal **leaves** are ¾" to 5" long and lance shaped with the attachment at the narrow end. Upper leaves are fewer in number, clasping and smaller in size. Pale blue **flowers** grow in an elongated spike. Each flower is about ¾" to 1½" long. **Seedpods** are woolly. **Blooms** June to August. **Occurs** in central and southern Utah, Arizona, Colorado, and Nevada. Found in sandy soils on rocky uplands, hills, or benches in sagebrush, pinyon juniper woodlands, and Douglas fir communities. (5,500 to 9,000 ft)

COMMENTS: It is usually seen in the central and northern portions of Capitol Reef. Type locality for this species is on the Aquarius Plateau west of Capitol Reef. It also occurs in Bryce Canyon, Bears Ears, Glen Canyon, Canyonlands, and Zion.

LOA PENSTEMON

Penstemon ophianthus | **Plantago Family** Plantaginaceae

A perennial herb up to 16" tall with few to many erect **stems**. Foliage and stems are typically gray green in color and may be sticky with glands. **Leaves** are 1" to 3" long, up to ⅜" wide, entire, lance shaped or linear. Leaf margins may be wavy or slightly toothed. Basal leaves grow on a short stalk, upper leaves are clasping and smaller in size. Leaves may be smooth without glands on the undersides. Blue lavender to blue violet **flowers** grow in a congested spike. Each flower is about ¾" to 1" long and has purple stripes running lengthwise along the swollen floral tube. Flowers extend outward when in full bloom. **Seeds** are inconspicuous. **Blooms** mid May to July. **Occurs** in central and southern Utah, Colorado, Arizona, and New Mexico. Found in sandy soils on canyon bottoms, hills, or benches in mixed desert scrub, sagebrush, pinyon juniper woodlands, and ponderosa pine communities. (5,300 to 7,800 ft)

COMMENTS: It can be found throughout Capitol Reef, and in Arches.

Synonyms: Penstemon jamesii subsp. ophianthus

MUSSENTUCHIT GILIA

Aliciella tenuis | **Phlox Family** Polemoniaceae

A long-lived perennial that ranges from 2" to 11" tall. Plant base is commonly branched and covered with brown, withered leaf bases. **Stems** and leaves are covered with tiny glands that collect grains of sand. Basal **leaves** are up to 3" long, about ⅓" wide, and spatula to narrowly lance shaped; they may be toothed, pinnately lobed, or entire with tiny pointed spines. There are few leaves on the stems and these are much reduced in size. Pale blue or lavender **flowers** are usually solitary and growing from the branch ends. They are tubular and up to ¾" long with flaring petal lobes. **Blooms** May to June. **Occurs** only in south central Utah. Found in mixed desert scrub, mountain brush, and pinyon juniper woodland communities. (5,700 to 9,000 ft)

COMMENTS: A few populations occur in Capitol Reef. Since it is an extremely rare Colorado Plateau endemic, it is a National Park Service sensitive species currently being monitored by Capitol Reef staff.

FLOCCOSE GILIA

Gilia inconspicua | **Phlox Family** Polemoniaceae

A delicate annual that grows up to 17" tall, but is more typically seen much shorter. Foliage is covered with sticky hairs and glands. Basal **leaves** are up to 3" long and deeply lobed with indentations more than halfway to the midrib. Leaves are much reduced in size on the upper stem. The tiny, blue to lavender or whitish **flowers** are borne in flat or rounded topped terminal clusters. **Seeds** are inconspicuous. **Blooms** April to July. **Occurs** in central and southern Utah, Arizona, New Mexico, and California. Found in sagebrush, mixed desert scrub, pinyon juniper woodland, and warm desert scrub communities. (2,500 to 7,500 ft)

COMMENTS: This delicate wildflower is widespread in the southern portions of Capitol Reef, often seen along the Notom Road in early spring. It also occurs in Arches, Canyonlands, Bears Ears, Glen Canyon, and Zion.

Synonyms: Ipomopsis inconspicua

BLUE TRUMPETS

Ipomopsis longiflora | **Phlox Family** Polemoniaceae

An annual that grows up to 2' tall. Plants typically have multiple branching **stems**. Threadlike **leaves** are 1" to 2" long and grow all along the stems. Foliage may be smooth or densely covered with fine hairs. The delicate pale blue **flowers** are up to 2" long, with a long, narrow tube and five flared petal lobes that bend at a right angle to the tube. Flowers are solitary or in pairs. **Seeds** are inconspicuous. **Blooms** May to November. **Occurs** in southern Utah, Texas, Arizona, and Colorado to South Dakota. Found in sandy soils on benches and uplands in mixed desert scrub, sagebrush, and pinyon juniper woodlands. (3,000 to 8,000 ft)

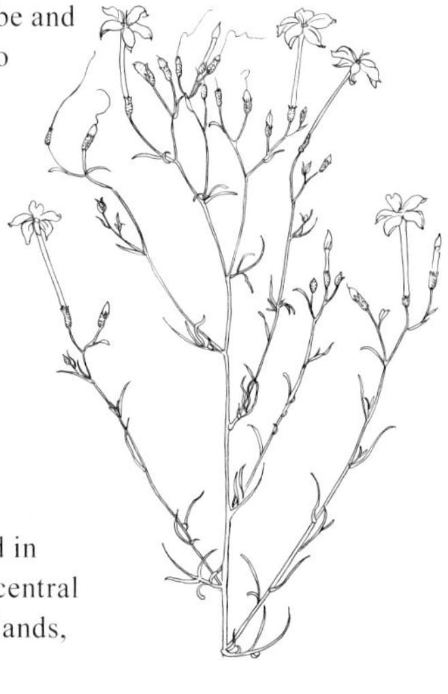

COMMENTS: American Indians have many medicinal uses for this plant, including an ointment to treat body sores and to reduce fevers. In Arizona, this species is often found in limestone soils. This delicate wildflower is found in washes and canyon bottoms in the northern and central portions of Capitol Reef, and in Arches, Canyonlands, Glen Canyon, Grand Staircase, and Zion.

DWARF GILIA

Ipomopsis pumila | **Phlox Family** Polemoniaceae

An annual that grows between 1" and 9" tall. Plants have simple **stems** or ones that branch near the base. Most of the **leaves** are on the stems. Leaves are entire, or may have three to seven lobes; indentations extend to more than half the distance to the leaf midrib. The tiny white to pale lavender **flowers** may be few to numerous in leafy terminal clusters. The floral tube is only about ⅓" long. **Seeds** are inconspicuous. **Blooms** April to June. **Occurs** in southern and central Utah, New Mexico, Arizona, Texas, and Colorado. Found in sagebrush, saltbush, and pinyon juniper woodlands. (4,500 to 7,000 ft)

COMMENTS: This tiny wildflower is found on the uplands and benches in the central and southern portions of Capitol Reef. It also occurs in Arches, Canyonlands, and Glen Canyon.

Synonyms: Gilia pumila

LONGLEAF PHLOX

Phlox longifolia | **Phlox Family** Polemoniaceae

An herbaceous perennial 2" to 16" tall that grows either with solitary stems or in compact clumps. **Stems** are covered with long, shaggy hairs. **Leaves** are linear to lance or egg shaped and ⅜" to 3" long. The pink, white, or lavender **flowers** are borne in open, terminal clusters, are ⅜" to ¾" across, and have five flaring lobes. **Seeds** are inconspicuous. **Blooms** April to July. **Occurs** throughout Utah, Arizona, and California and north to Canada. Found in sagebrush, mixed desert scrub, saltbush scrub, pinyon juniper woodland, ponderosa pine, spruce fir, and aspen communities. (4,400 to 9,600 ft)

COMMENTS: This delicate wildflower can be seen in the northern and central portions of Capitol Reef, including Cathedral Valley and Cedar Mesa. It also occurs in Bryce Canyon, Bears Ears, Canyonlands, Grand Staircase, and Zion.

ALCOVE OR CAVE PRIMROSE

Primula specuicola | **Primrose Family** Primulaceae

A long-lived herbaceous perennial, 3" to 10" tall. **Leaves** are spatula shaped with slightly dentate or toothed margins. They are gray-green in color on the upper side slightly whitish below. Pale lavender **flowers** grow in clusters of ten to 25 atop a central stem; each flower has a tube about ⅜" long with petals (⅜" to ½" across) that flare broadly at the top. Brown **seed** pods are elliptical, up to ¾" long. **Blooms** April to June. **Occurs** in southern Utah and Arizona. Found in hanging gardens and moist seep areas in sandstone canyon alcoves. (3,300 to 6,750 ft)

COMMENTS: An uncommon Colorado Plateau endemic found in the very southern portions of Capitol Reef, and in Arches, Canyonlands, and Glen Canyon. The name *Primula* comes from Latin meaning "early spring," referencing the early blooming time, and *specuicola* is Latin for "cave." These plants cling to sandstone walls in alcoves in very fragile substrates; do not try to walk or climb right up to them as you can easily destroy their home!

Synonyms: Primula hunnewellii

COLORADO COLUMBINE

Aquilegia caerulea | **Buttercup Family** Ranunculaceae

A perennial herb 6" to 24" tall with primarily basal leaves and slender **stems**. Plants tend to have few or no glands or hairs on the leaves and stems. This is one of the diagnostic features for distinguishing different species in this genus. Basal **leaves** are up to 15" long and two to three times divided with rounded lobes. Foliage tends to be a deep green color with the underside of leaves being slightly lighter. One to several showy, pale blue to whitish **flowers** grow on bare slender stalks. Each flower has a long claw extending down from the base. **Seeds** are inconspicuous. **Blooms** July to August. **Occurs** throughout Utah, Idaho, and Montana south to Arizona and New Mexico. It typically grows in cool, shady locations, or moist areas within sagebrush, pinyon juniper woodlands, and Douglas fir forests. (5,500 to 12,000 ft)

COMMENTS: It can be found in the northern portion of Capitol Reef. It also occurs in Bryce Canyon, Cedar Breaks, and Zion. This is the Colorado state wildflower. The genus name, *Aquilegia*, comes from the Latin word for "eagle," referring to the petal claw. American Indians used plants within this genus as perfumes.

ROCKY MOUNTAIN CLEMATIS

Clematis columbiana | **Buttercup Family** Ranunculaceae

A vine-like or trailing perennial herb. This plant may spread out along the ground, or sprawl over shrubs and through trees. Opposite, compound **leaves** grow on short stalks and are two or three times divided, with toothed or lobed margins. Blue or lavender, nodding **flowers** are solitary on long stalks. There are no petals, only petal-like, showy sepals that are 1½" long. **Seeds** are showy feathery plumes dispersed by the wind. **Blooms** May to late June. **Occurs** throughout much of Utah and Montana, and south to Arizona and New Mexico. Found in sandy soils in sagebrush, ponderosa pine, aspen, and spruce fir woodlands. (6,000 to 10,800 ft)

COMMENTS: This plant grows best when its roots are in shady, protected niches, but the rest of the plant gets full sun during much of the day. It is often seen growing in sandstone crevices in our area. Found in the northern portions of Capitol Reef, and in Bryce Canyon, Canyonlands, Cedar Breaks, Bears Ears, and Zion.

ANDERSON'S LARKSPUR

Delphinium andersonii | **Buttercup Family** Ranunculaceae

A perennial herb 6" to 24" tall with primarily basal leaves and slender, erect **stems**. **Leaves** on stems are much reduced, few in number and have smooth foliage without hairs and glands. Basal leaves, ⅜" to 2⅜" long, are typically divided three times. One to fifteen showy, blue to whitish **flowers** grow on an elongated stalk. Each flower has a long spur extending down from the base and five petal-like sepals also bluish in color. **Seeds** are inconspicuous. **Blooms** mid May to July. **Occurs** in southern Utah, Colorado, Arizona, and New Mexico. Found in mixed desert scrub, saltbush, and pinyon juniper woodlands. (2,800 to 7,100 ft)

COMMENTS: Most often seen in the northern portion of Capitol Reef, however during good bloom years it can be seen along the Notom Road. It also occurs in Bryce Canyon and Zion. The genus name, *Delphinium*, means "like a Dolphin," which refers to the shape of the flower bud. This plant also contains a glycoside, delphinidin, and several alkaloids that are very toxic to livestock. American Indians and early pioneers used plants in this genus to kill body lice. All parts of the plants should be considered poisonous.

Synonyms: Delphinium cognatum, Delphinium scaposum var. andersonii, Delphinium xylorrhizum

SILVER-LEAF NIGHTSHADE

Solanum elaeagnifolium **Potato Family** Solanaceae

A non-native, herbaceous perennial that reaches 3' tall, but typically seen about 18" tall. It grows from deep, thick, underground spreading rootstalks. The entire plant is covered with fine hairs, giving it a silvery appearance. Alternate **leaves** are somewhat heart shaped and deeply lobed near the base (2" to 5" long). The midrib of each leaf has short yellow spines on it, making this a prickly plant to touch. Showy purple to bluish **flowers** grow in clusters on short stalks. Five petals appear flattened or wide open; about ¾" to 1" across. Stamens are bright yellow. **Fruit** is a red to brownish round berry about ½" in diameter. Each berry is filled with tiny seeds. **Blooms** May to September. **Occurs** from Washington south through California and east through Arizona, New Mexico and southern Utah to North Carolina. Native to Eurasia. Found in disturbed soils, especially in areas that have experienced heavy grazing pressure. (5,200 to 7,000 ft)

COMMENTS: This species can be seen in the Hickman Bridge parking lot in Capitol Reef. It also occurs in Glen Canyon, Zion, and Bears Ears. It is toxic to livestock and should be considered highly toxic to humans as well. Several Puebloan tribes use different parts of the plant for medicinal purposes such as treating wounds and toothaches. They also used crushed dried berries to curdle milk for making cheeses.

Synonyms: Solanum flavidum

PINK TO RED FLOWERS

SAN JUAN ONION

Allium macropetalum | **Lily Family** Liliaceae

A small lily, about 6" tall, with a main stalk and two leaves growing from a bulb buried 1" to 6" in the ground. Plants typically have two **leaves** (about 1/8" wide) that are semi-round in shape and extend above the main stalk. Bulbs are usually clustered together (as in the photo) and reach about 2¼" in diameter. A network of mesh veined fibrous scales surrounds the bulb. This meshing is often several layers thick. Two to three **bracts** (with three to five veins) subtend the **flower** cluster. Flower umbel contains few to numerous pink to whitish flowers. Each flower has a purple mid vein. **Seeds** are tiny inconspicuous capsules. **Blooms** April to July. **Occurs** in south central Utah, Colorado, Arizona, Texas, and New Mexico. Typically grows in sandy soils on rocky benches in saltbush, desert scrub, and pinyon juniper woodlands. (3,700 to 6,300 ft)

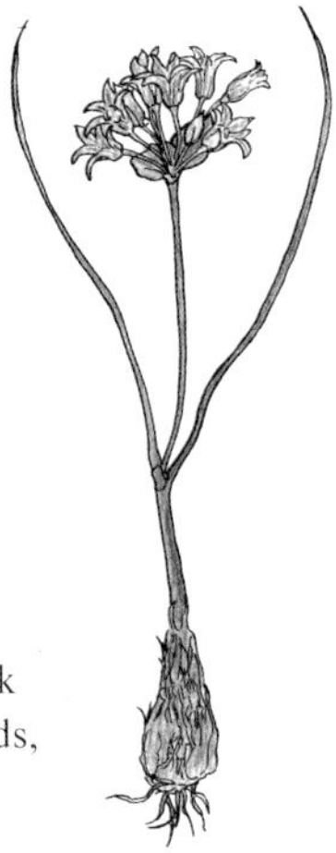

COMMENTS: Found in the central and southern portions of Capitol Reef, often seen in the Hall's Creek area. It also occurs in Arches, Bears Ears, Canyonlands, Grand Staircase, and Glen Canyon.

Synonyms: Allium reticulatum var. deserticola

ROUND LEAF OR PALLID MILKWEED

Asclepias cryptoceras | **Dogbane Family** Apocynaceae

A low, sprawling, stout, herbaceous perennial 4" to 12" tall. **Leaves** are round to oval, 1½" to 3" broad, and grow in opposite pairs along the stem. **Flowers** that grow in a cluster, from a short stalk up to 2¾" long, are comprised of greenish yellow petals and red purple, bag-shaped hoods at the center of each flower. **Seed** capsules are spindle shaped, 1½" to 2½" long and ½" to 1" broad, with a smooth surface. **Blooms** April to June. **Occurs** throughout Utah, Colorado, California, Wyoming, and Arizona. Commonly found in sandy, dry, shallow soils on rocky hills, benches, or mesas in desert scrub, grassland, or pinyon juniper communities. (3,700 to 6,500 ft)

COMMENTS: It is most commonly associated with Moenkopi, Entrada or Chinle formations and can be found scattered throughout Capitol Reef. This species also occurs in Arches, Bears Ears, Grand Staircase, and Glen Canyon. Milkweeds contain cardiac glycosides known to be poisonous to both humans and livestock. Poisoning symptoms from cardiac glycosides include dullness, weakness, bloating, inability to stand or walk, high body temperatures, rapid and weak pulse, difficulty breathing, dilated pupils, spasms, and coma. *Asclepias* comes from the name of the Greek God of medicine, Asklepio.

CUTLER'S MILKWEED

Asclepias cutleri | **Dogbane Family** Apocynaceae

A small, herbaceous perennial that reaches 7" in height on slender **stems**. This delicate milkweed initially appears to be an annual. **Leaves** are nearly sessile, very narrow and 1" to 3" long. Herbage is gray green in color. **Flowers** grow in dense clusters at stem ends, with each flower on its own short stalk. Each cluster of flowers is about 1" in diameter. Flowers are rose to purple colored with white hoods. **Seed** pods are 1" to 3" long, narrow and spindle shaped. **Blooms** April to June. **Occurs** in northern Arizona, southern Utah, east to New Mexico and southwestern Colorado. (4,000 to 5,500 ft)

COMMENTS: This species is a rare endemic that occurs only in the Colorado Plateau. It has yet to be recorded in Capitol Reef, but can be seen in sand dunes and sandy soils within Bears Ears.

RUTH'S MILKWEED

Asclepias ruthiae | **Dogbane Family** Apocynaceae

A small, low growing herbaceous perennial that has few branching stems. Both **stems** and leaves are covered with tiny white matted hairs, giving the plant a grayish green appearance. **Leaves** are broadly oval to heart shaped (3/8" to 1¼" long and the same wide). Small pale violet to rose purple **flowers** bloom from branch tips. **Seed** capsules are broadly spindle shaped, hanging down from short pedicels, 1¼" to 1½" long and ½" wide, with smooth surfaces. **Blooms** late April to June. **Occurs** only in central and eastern Utah and northern Arizona. Found in mixed desert scrub, saltbush, and pinyon juniper communities. It typically grows in dry, sandy soils on hills, benches, or bottomlands. (4,500 to 5,900 ft)

COMMENTS: Due to its limited distribution, lack of known occurrences, and small population sizes, Ruth's milkweed is considered a rare endemic and is a National Park Service sensitive species. State and federal botanists are watching this species to determine if there are any long-term threats. Only a few individual plants have been found Capitol Reef, Arches and Canyonlands.

Synonyms: Asclepias eastwoodiana, Asclepias uncialis var. ruthiae

SHOWY MILKWEED

Asclepias speciosa | **Dogbane Family** Apocynaceae

A tall (23" to 40"), stout stemmed, simply branched herbaceous perennial. Both leaves and **stems** are densely covered with white woolly hairs. **Leaves** grow in opposite pairs on the stem, are elliptical to oval shaped and up to 8" long and 1¼" to 5½" wide. Rose purple **flowers** form large round balls at the top of the plant and are quite showy. The out-curving pink <u>hoods</u> are raised slightly above the flower base. **Seed** capsules are erect, broadly spindle shaped, 3½" to 4¾" long and ¾" to 1¼" wide. They are densely spiny and completely covered with woolly, white hairs. **Blooms** May to August. **Occurs** throughout Utah, and is widespread throughout the southwest, to California, Canada, and Minnesota. It is often seen in weedy, disturbed places such as old agricultural fields, but also occurs in moist, sandy bottomlands or riparian strips. (2,700 to 9,000 ft)

COMMENTS: Found in bottomlands and orchards within the central portion of Capitol Reef. It also occurs in Arches, Canyonlands, Bears Ears, Bryce Canyon, and Zion. As with all milkweeds, this plant should be considered poisonous, although it is not as deadly as some species. According to American Indian herbal lore, some portions of Showy milkweed were used to stimulate kidney function and aid in clearing up bronchial infections. During World War II, milkweed pods were harvested throughout the United States for the fluff within each pod. This fluff was discovered as being five to six times as buoyant as cork, much lighter weight than wool, and much warmer. Life jackets were filled with milkweed fluff and flight suits for pilots were lined with fluff to act as a life preserver if the pilot fell in the ocean.

JONES' CYCLADENIA

Cycladenia humilis var. jonesii | **Dogbane Family** Apocynaceae

An herbaceous perennial that grows to 14" tall. **Leaves** are thick and fleshy, have no hairs, but are covered with a whitish waxy coating. They are 1⅓" to nearly 4" long, ¾" to 2½" wide, oval to broadly rounded in shape. **Flowers** are rose pink in color; about 1" long and up to 1¼" wide. Flowers have two forms depending on the population site; they may large and broadly opening or smaller and narrowly opening. **Seedpods** are up to 3¾" long, fairly narrow and contain numerous tiny brown seeds. **Blooms** May to June. **Occurs** only in south central Utah. Found in saline soils in mixed desert scrub and juniper woodlands communities. (4,400 to 6,600 ft)

COMMENTS: This is a federally listed threatened species fully protected by law. Type locality is north of the Waterpocket Fold, Utah. It is found in the southern portion of Capitol Reef, Grand Staircase, and Glen Canyon.

Synonyms: Cycladenia jonesii

WAVY LEAFED THISTLE

Cirsium undulatum | **Sunflower Family** Asteraceae

An herbaceous perennial reaching 3' tall, with erect, white woolly **stems**. Foliage is covered with gray hairs. **Leaves** are primarily basal, grayish, and up to 8" long. They are toothed or lobed, tipped with yellow spines, and covered with gray hairs on both sides. **Flowers** grow in a terminal flower head about 2" wide. Pink flowers grow from an urn shaped cup that has spiny bracts. **Seeds** are showy white plumes. **Blooms** June to September. **Occurs** throughout much of Utah to Canada, Minnesota, Missouri, Arizona, and New Mexico. Found in mixed desert scrub, sagebrush, and juniper woodlands often in disturbed soils along roadsides and in fields. (4,600 to 9,500 ft)

COMMENTS: Most commonly seen in the central portion of Capitol Reef around Fruita. It also occurs in Arches, Bryce Canyon, Canyonlands, Bears Ears, and Glen Canyon. Several American Indian tribes used this plant to treat venereal diseases; it was also used to treat burns and sores and as a remedy for diabetes. Early pioneers used it as a tonic and diuretic.

Synonyms: Cnicus undulatus

MOUND DAISY

Erigeron compactus | **Sunflower Family** Asteraceae

An herbaceous perennial only 3" to 4" tall that grows as a cushion like mound. The lower **branches** are typically covered with dark brown shaggy bark. **Leaves** are mostly basal, less than an inch long, and very narrow and linear. They may be covered with tiny, soft hairs. **Flower heads** are solitary. Ray flowers are white to pink, about ½" across. When plant in full bloom it looks like a small white bouquet sitting on the ground. **Seeds** are inconspicuous. **Blooms** May to June. **Occurs** throughout Utah, Nevada, California, and Arizona. The variety found in Capitol Reef typically grows in semi-barren clay soils in desert scrub and pinyon juniper communities. (5,000 to 7,000 ft)

COMMENTS: Occasionally seen in the northern and central portions of Capitol Reef. This species closely resembles the Basin Daisy and can easily be confused with it. One way to differentiate them is that this species has essentially leafless stems.

SHOWY RUSHPINK

Lygodesmia grandiflora | **Sunflower Family** Asteraceae

An herbaceous perennial that has long underground stems. Plants grow 3" to 20" tall, typically with few to no **branches**, and are grayish green in color. **Leaves** are ¼" to 4" long and 1/16" to ¼" wide, entire, linear in shape, and reduced in size on the upper reaches of the stalk. Pink to pink purple **flower heads** are solitary on the stems; the entire flower head is about 1" to 1¼" across. Tiny **seeds** are attached to long, white hairs. **Blooms** mid May to August. **Occurs** in central and southern Utah to Arizona. Found in sandy soils on benches or in canyons in desert scrub, sagebrush, pinyon juniper, and ponderosa pine communities. (4,800 to 9,000 ft)

COMMENTS: The photo and line drawing depict the two varieties of this species confirmed to occur in Capitol Reef. Fairly common in the northern and central portions of Capitol Reef after good winter precipitation. It also occurs in Arches, Bryce Canyon, Canyonlands, Glen Canyon, Grand Staircase, and Zion.

Synonyms: Erythremia grandiflora, Lygodesmia grandiflora var. stricta

TANSYLEAF ASTER

Machaeranthera tanacetifolia | **Sunflower Family** Asteraceae

An erect, bushy annual that may reach up to 20" tall. Foliage is covered with long, soft hairs and occasional glandular hairs. **Stems** are erect and may be tinged with purple. **Leaves** are up to 3/8" to 2½" long and highly dissected to the midrib of each leaf, resembling fern leaves. Leaf lobes are tipped with spiny bristles. **Flower heads** are few to many in a flat or rounded topped cluster and are about ¾" wide. Ray flowers are pink to purple. Disk flowers are bright yellow. **Seeds** are woolly with hairs. **Blooms** mid April to October. **Occurs** throughout much of Utah. Found in mixed desert scrub, saltbush scrub, and pinyon juniper woodland communities. (2,800 to 6,000 ft)

COMMENTS: Most commonly seen in the central portion of Capitol Reef, but also found along the Notom Road in the south. It also occurs in Arches, Canyonlands, Glen Canyon, Grand Staircase, and Zion. The genus name, *Machaeranthera*, means "sickle anther," referring to the anther shape. The specific name, *tanacetifolia*, makes reference to the fernlike leaves.

Synonyms: Aster tanacetifolius, Chrysopsis coronopifolia, Machaeranthera coronopifolia

THORNY WIRELETTUCE

Stephanomeria spinosa | **Sunflower Family** Asteraceae

A spiny, herbaceous perennial with a woody base that reaches 20" tall. Base of older plant has dried leaves and branches from previous year's growth that are tan to brownish in color. **Stems** are much branched and widely spreading, giving the plant a tangled web appearance. Stems are covered with long spines. **Leaves** are up to 2¾" long on the lower branches; they are very narrow, linear and reduced in size on the upper reaches of the stalk. One tends to notice the spines before even looking for or seeing any leaves. Pink to pink purple **flower heads** are terminal and have three to five flowers each. The entire flower head is about ½" across. Tiny **seeds** are attached to long, white hairs that blow in away in the wind. **Blooms** July to September. **Occurs** throughout much of Utah and the western United States to British Columbia. Found in mixed desert scrub, sagebrush, pinyon juniper, and aspen communities. (5,500 to 10,000 ft)

COMMENTS: Fairly common in the northern and central portions of Capitol Reef, and in Bryce Canyon.

Synonyms: Lygodesmia spinosa

SLENDER WIRELETTUCE

Stephanomeria tenuifolia | **Sunflower Family** Asteraceae

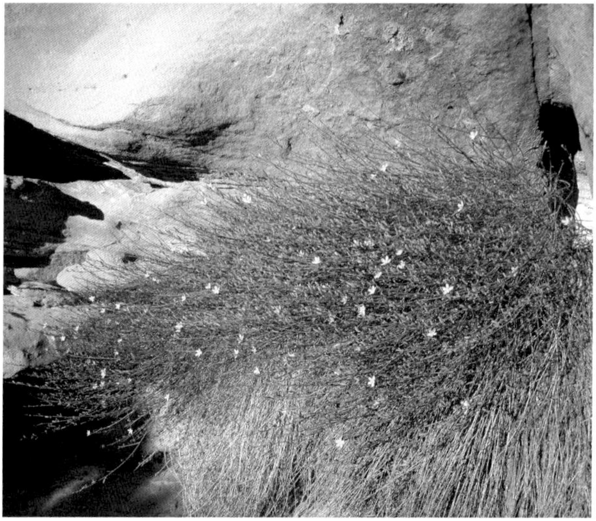

An herbaceous perennial that grows 10" to 40" tall. It is a scraggly shrub with numerous smooth, erect, green **branches**. **Leaves** are 3/8" to 3¼" long and narrow, linear in shape, and may be toothed. Leaves on the stems are much reduced upwards. Pale pink **flower heads** are borne at the end of short branches and are about ¾" across. Ray flowers are widely spaced and toothed at the end. **Seeds** are tiny, five-ribbed with bristly plumes. **Blooms** June to October. **Occurs** throughout much of Utah and the western United States. Found in desert scrub, sagebrush, pinyon juniper woodlands, ponderosa pine, and white fir communities. Occasionally found in hanging gardens in the Colorado Plateau region. (3,800 to 9,000 ft)

COMMENTS: Common throughout the central and southern portions of Capitol Reef. It also occurs in Arches, Canyonlands, Bryce Canyon, Bears Ears, Glen Canyon, and Zion. The genus name, *Stephanomeria,* is derived from the Greek word *stephane*, "wreath or crown," and *meros*, "division," which refers to the spacing between the ray flowers.

Synonyms: Lygodesmia wrightii, Ptiloria tenuifolia, Stephanomeria minor, Stephanomeria wrightii

WESTERN ASTER

Symphyotrichum ascendens | **Sunflower Family** Asteraceae

An herbaceous perennial with an underground, horizontal rootstalk system. Plants reach 5" to 36" tall. **Stems** and leaves are covered with stiff hairs. **Leaves** are 1¼" to 6" long and 1/16" to ½" wide, entire, with the upper ones becoming smaller and smaller. They are often deciduous when in full bloom. One to many flower heads form in a narrow cluster. Ray **flowers** are purplish to pink, 1" to 1¼" across. Tiny **seeds** are covered with white woolly hairs. **Blooms** July to November. **Occurs** throughout Utah to Canada and south to New Mexico. It typically grows in shallow, moist, sandy soils on alluvial fans/washes in desert scrub, riparian, sagebrush, pinyon juniper, and ponderosa pine woodlands. (3,900 to 8,900 ft)

COMMENTS: Common in the central portion of Capitol Reef, and in Arches, Canyonlands, Bryce Canyon, Cedar Breaks, Bears Ears, Zion, and Glen Canyon.

Synonyms: Aster adscendens, Aster chilensis subsp. adscendens

BARNEBY REED-MUSTARD

Schoenocrambe barnebyi | **Mustard Family** Brassicaceae

An herbaceous perennial reaching 4" to 10" tall. Herbage is glabrous or may be covered with small, coarse fine hairs. **Leaves** are ½" to 1" long, 1/16" to 7/8" wide, oblong to elliptic, growing on short stalks. They may be entire or slightly toothed, but are not heart shaped. Leaf ends are rounded. **Flowers** grow on an elongated stalk with two to 28 flowers. They are ascending to spreading. Sepals are ¼" long, green to violet, with papery margins. Petals are up to ½" long, narrow, and white to lavender with conspicuous purplish veins. **Seedpods** are up to 2¼" long, very narrow, and ascending to spreading. **Blooms** late April to mid June. **Occurs** only in south central Utah. Found in mixed desert scrub and open pinyon juniper woodlands. (5,400 to 5,800 ft)

COMMENTS: This is a Colorado Plateau endemic that is federally listed as Endangered and is protected by law. It occurs in Capitol Reef.

LITTLE TWISTFLOWER

Streptanthella longirostris | **Mustard Family** Brassicaceae

An annual growing 10" to 20" tall with erect branches. **Stems** have many branches; foliage is bluish green. **Leaves** are ½" to 3" long and up to ⅓" wide, lance shaped to elliptical, with the lower ones being lobed to entire. **Flowers** are two toned, with greenish to purple sepals and white veined magenta petals. They grow along the entirety of the stalk, blooming first at the lower end and gradually progressing to the tip. Flowers are fairly small and urn shaped. **Seedpods** are long and slender, up to 2½" long, bending downwards. **Blooms** April to June. **Occurs** throughout Utah, New Mexico, and Wyoming. Found in sandy to gravelly soils in mixed desert scrub and pinyon juniper woodland communities; common on uplands, benches and in canyon bottoms. (4,000 to 7,000 ft)

COMMENTS: It is widespread throughout Capitol Reef, and in Arches, Canyonlands, Bryce Canyon, Bears Ears, Glen Canyon, Grand Staircase, and Zion.

Synonyms: Arabis longirostris, Thelypodium longirostre

HEARTLEAF TWISTFLOWER

Streptanthus cordatus | **Mustard Family** Brassicaceae

An herbaceous perennial growing 12" to 20" tall with smooth, erect branches. Typically few **stems** with little or no branching; foliage is bluish green. Basal **leaves** ¾" to 3" long and up to 1" wide, heart shaped with toothed to entire margins. Leaves clasp the stems, are oval to heart shaped, and reduce in size up the stem. **Flowers** are urn shaped with the tips of the yellow to purple sepals pinching inwards on the magenta petals. Flowers grow along the entirety of the stalk, blooming first at the lower end and gradually progressing to the tip. **Seedpods** are narrow but flattened, up to 3" long, and curve upwards. **Blooms** April to July. **Occurs** throughout Utah, north to Oregon, Wyoming, California, and Nevada. Found in mixed desert scrub, blackbrush, sagebrush, shadscale, pinyon juniper woodland up to Douglas fir communities. (3,500 to 9,700 ft)

COMMENTS: Usually seen in the central and northern portions of Capitol Reef, and in Arches, Canyonlands, Bryce Canyon, Bears Ears, Glen Canyon, Grand Staircase, and Zion. The genus name, *Streptanthus,* is Greek for "twisted flower." The specific name, *cordatus,* also Greek, means "heartlike," referring to the leaves.

LONGLEAF SNOWBERRY

Symphoricarpos longiflorus | **Honeysuckle Family** Caprifoliaceae

A large, sprawling shrub 3' tall with numerous intricate branches. New **branches** are usually smooth, while the older branches turn brown and have shredded bark. Opposite **leaves** are simple, rounded, and a light blue green. Leaves are thin, about ½" long, and 1/3" wide, oval to lance shaped, and have entire margins. Pale to bright pink **flowers** are tubular, about ½" in length, and usually occur in pairs. They are very fragrant. Petal lobes are much shorter than the tube. **Fruits** are white, waxy berries (not palatable to humans). **Blooms** May to August. **Occurs** throughout Utah, Oregon, California, Arizona, Texas, and New Mexico. Found in mixed desert scrub, sagebrush, pinyon juniper, ponderosa pine woodlands, and hanging garden communities. (3,000 to 9,500 ft)

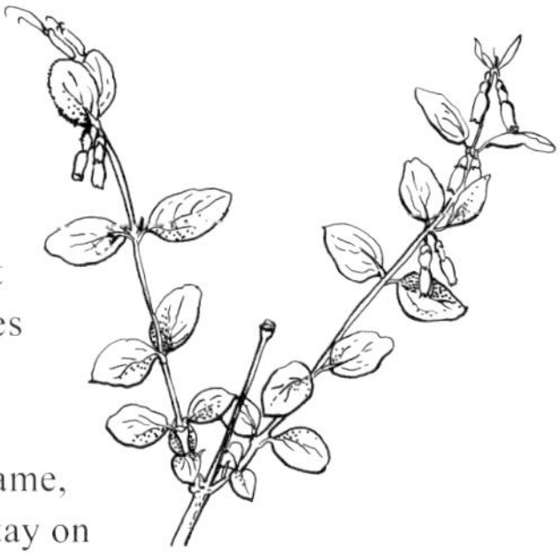

COMMENTS: It is found throughout Capitol Reef, typically along washes and in canyon bottoms. It also occurs in Arches, Canyonlands, Bears Ears, Glen Canyon, Grand Staircase, and Zion. American Indians used the roots of this plant to treat colds and stomachaches, although the leaves contain a poisonous drug. This plant is valuable forage for several species of wildlife and the dense stands create good cover for birds. The common name, snowberry, refers to the white, waxy berries that stay on the shrub for a long time in the fall.

ROCKY MOUNTAIN BEE PLANT

Peritoma serrulata | **Spider Plant Family** Cleomaceae

An erect annual that grows to 3' tall. Plant may be single stemmed or have a few branching **stems**, typically without hairs. **Leaves** have three leaflets that are elliptic to lance shaped, ¼" to 2¾" long and 1/8" to 3/8" wide. **Flowering** stalks are up to 10" tall with erect, stout, with purple pink flowers. **Seeds** form within a pod 1" to 2¾" long. **Blooms** April to October. **Occurs** throughout Utah, north to Canada, California, and Arizona. Found in disturbed sites such as roadsides, old fields, or disturbed bottomlands. (3,000 to 9,000 ft)

COMMENTS: Seen mostly in the central and northern portions of Capitol Reef, and in Canyonlands, Zion and Bears Ears. This species was commonly used by American Indians as food, and as a dye for coloring clay pots. It is recognized as an indictor of prehistoric sites in the Pueblo Province.

Synonyms: Cleome serrulata

CRESCENT MILKVETCH

Astragalus amphioxys | **Pea Family** Fabaceae

An erect perennial growing 2" to 14" tall. Foliage is covered with stiff hairs. Compound **leaves** are up to 1 ½" long, with five to 21 oblong or egg shaped leaflets up to ¾" long and ¼" wide. **Flower** stalks may surpass the leafy branches up to 8" and have two to 13 flowers per stalk. The pink purple flowers curve upwards at full bloom. They are about ½" to 1" long. **Seedpods** curve upwards, are sessile or nearly so, crescent shaped (1 ½" long and less than 3/8" wide), and covered with soft spreading hairs. **Blooms** March to June. **Occurs** in southern Utah, Arizona, Nevada, and New Mexico. Found in sandy soils in mixed desert scrub, and pinyon juniper communities. (2,200 to 6,600 ft)

COMMENTS: Found in the central and southern portions of Capitol Reef. Large fields of this species may be seen in the vicinity of Hanksville, Utah during good bloom years. It also occurs in Arches, Bryce Canyon, Canyonlands, Grand Staircase, and Zion.

PAINTED MILKVETCH

Astragalus ceramicus | **Pea Family** Fabaceae

A small, sprawling perennial with **stems** 1" to 16" long. Foliage is covered with tiny hairs. Compound **leaves** are up to 6" long, with three to 13 linear leaflets up to 1" long and very narrow. **Flower** stalks have two to 15 flowers. The purple to pinkish flowers have bell shaped sepals. Flowers are about ¼" to ½" long. **Seedpods** are pendulous, borne on a short stalk, oval to egg shaped and mottled with reddish blotches. **Blooms** late April to June. **Occurs** throughout Utah, Arizona, Idaho, Montana, Oklahoma, and New Mexico. Found in sandy soils in mixed desert scrub, sagebrush, near stream banks and in pinyon juniper communities. (4,200 to 8,000 ft)

COMMENTS: Commonly found in the central and northern portions of Capitol Reef. It also occurs in Arches, Canyonlands, Bears Ears, Glen Canyon, Grand Staircase, and Zion. The specific name, *ceramicus*, refers to the pod's shiny appearance, which makes it look like fired ceramic.

COLTON'S MILKVETCH

Astragalus coltonii | **Pea Family** Fabaceae

A rush-like perennial herb that grows to 30" tall. **Stems** are erect or ascending, covered with fine hairs. Compound **leaves** are between ¾" and 4" long with three to 19 leaflets up to ¾" long and less than 1/16" wide. Leaflets are linear to oval and hairy on both sides. **Flower** stalk is up to 11" long, with each stalk having six to 30 flowers. The tiny, ¾" long flowers are pink purple and spread outward from the stalk at full bloom. The calyx is purplish and covered with tiny black hairs. **Seedpods** are declining and straight or nearly so, oblong to lance shaped, and strongly laterally compressed. They are about 11/3" long, and smooth. One of the key features to distinguish this species is the laterally compressed pods. (*Astragalus harrisonii*, which grows alongside *A. coltonii*, has pods that are dorsi-ventrally compressed.) Pods have a single seed compartment. **Blooms** May to June. **Occurs** only in south central Utah. Found in mixed desert scrub and pinyon juniper woodlands. (4,800 to 7,500 ft)

COMMENTS: Found in the northern and central portions of Capitol Reef. This species closely resembles several other rushlike *Astragalus* species, making final identification challenging. This species also occurs in Arches, Canyonlands, Bears Ears, and Glen Canyon.

BISHOP'S MILKVETCH

Astragalus episcopus | **Pea Family** Fabaceae

A rush-like perennial herb that grows to 18" tall. **Stems** are erect or ascending, and covered with fine hairs. Compound **leaves** are between ¾" to 4" long with three to 13 leaflets up to 5/8" long and less than 1/16" wide. Leaflets are linear to elliptical and hairy on both sides. **Flower** stalk is up to 9" long, with each stalk having six to 30 flowers. The tiny 5/8" long flowers are pink purple and curve upwards at full bloom. **Seedpods** are declining and straight or nearly so, sessile or nearly so, and typically oblong in shape. They are ½" to 1¼" long, and may be covered with long hairs. **Blooms** May to June. **Occurs** only in south central Utah, Arizona and New Mexico. Found in silty clay to clay soils in mixed desert scrub and pinyon juniper woodlands. (4,100 to 6,100 ft)

COMMENTS: It is most commonly seen the South Desert and Cathedral Valley areas in Capitol Reef. It also occurs in Canyonlands.

CLAY MILKVETCH

Astragalus flavus var. argillosus | **Pea Family** Fabaceae

A short-lived perennial growing 2" to 12" tall. Plants are erect as a small cluster of branches with flowers at the terminal branch ends. They are strongly scented plants. Compound **leaves** are up to 6" long, with nine to 21 oblong or linear leaflets that are ¼" to 1" long and very narrow. Plants are covered with stiff greenish hairs. **Flower** stalks extend above the leafy branches; stalks have six to 30 flowers. The pink purple flowers curve upwards at full bloom and quickly fade to a cream color. They are about ½" to ¾" long and the flower tube is bell shaped and woolly with hairs. **Seedpods** curve upwards, are sessile or nearly so, oblong in shape, and are ¼" to ½" long and about 1/8" wide. They are nearly straight and may be covered with soft spreading hairs. **Blooms** April to July and again in the fall after good rainfall. **Occurs** in southern Utah, Arizona, Nevada, New Mexico, Colorado, and Wyoming. The pink flowered variety (var. *argillosus*) is endemic to southern Utah. Found in saline, clay soils in salt desert scrub and pinyon juniper woodlands. (4,000 to 5,700 ft)

COMMENTS: This species comes in three varieties; one of which has pink purple flowers, the other two have yellow flowers. Two of the varieties, var. *argillosus* (pink flowers) and var. *flavus* (yellowish flowers) occur in the central and northern desert portions of Capitol Reef. *A. flavus* also occurs in Bryce, Cedar Breaks, and Zion. This species is highly poisonous to livestock.

HARRISON'S MILKVETCH

Astragalus harrisonii | **Pea Family** Fabaceae

A perennial herb that grows into a moderate sized scruffy looking bush. Clumps may reach 24" in height and 36" in width. **Stems** are intricately branched and tangled. Branch internodes have small, distinct leaf-like appendages. Compound **leaves** are ⅝" to 2½" long with three to nine leaflets that are ⅜" long and 1/16" wide. The end leaflet is wider and blends into the main leaf axis. Leaflets are linear and hairy on both sides. **Flower** stalk is 2½" to 7½" tall and each stalk has three to 15 flowers. The ⅜" long flowers are pink purple, and curve upwards at full bloom. Corolla tube is bell shaped. Calyx is covered with short white hairs. (Similar species have short black hairs.) **Seedpods** hang down, are nearly straight, and are roundish in cross section. One of the key features to distinguish this species from look-alikes is the dorsi-ventrally compressed pods. (*Astragalus coltonii,* that grows with *A. harrisonii*, has pods that are laterally compressed.) Pods are ¾" to 1" long and may or may not be covered with hairs. They have a single seed compartment. **Blooms** late April to June. **Occurs** only in Wayne County, Utah. Harrison's milkvetch is found in pinyon juniper woodland and mixed desert scrub communities in Navajo and Kayenta formations. (5,400 to 5,600 ft)

COMMENTS: This species is a very rare endemic that occurs only in Capitol Reef and is a National Park Service sensitive species.

PRICKLY MILKVETCH

Astragalus kentrophyta | **Pea Family** Fabaceae

A perennial herb that grows along the ground with creeping stems. Plants often form mats that cover an area several feet across. **Stems** are prostrate to erect, covered with fine hairs. Compound **leaves** are between ⅛" to 1" long with three to nine leaflets up to ½" long and less than 1/16" wide. Leaflets are linear, spine tipped, and hairy on both sides. **Flower** stalk is up to ¾" long, with each stalk having one to three flowers. The tiny, ⅜" long flowers are purple to whitish and decline downwards at full bloom. **Seedpods** are declining and curved, sessile or nearly so, and typically are oblong in shape. They are up to ⅜" long, and covered with long hairs. **Blooms** May to September. **Occurs** throughout much of Utah, California, Oregon, Washington, Idaho, and New Mexico. Found in a variety of soil types in mixed desert scrub, pinyon juniper, and ponderosa pine woodlands. (3,200 to 12,000 ft)

COMMENTS: Commonly seen in the central and northern portions of Capitol Reef, and in Bryce Canyon, Cedar Breaks, Glen Canyon, and Canyonlands.

FRECKLED MILKVETCH

Astragalus lentiginosus | **Pea Famil**y Fabaceae

A perennial herb 6" to 24" tall. It often forms a scraggly clump with erect or reclining **stems**. Foliage is covered with short stiff hairs. Compound **leaves** are 1" to 6" long, with nine to 23 leaflets up to 7/8" long, and ovate to elliptical or lance shaped. **Flower** stalks are up to 6" long; each stalk has 11 to 30 flowers. The purple to cream colored flowers are erect to declining at full bloom. They are nearly 1" long and hairy. **Seedpods** may hang down or tip upright and are inflated in an oval shape about 1" to 1¼" long. Pods may be hairy or smooth, mottled or plain, and stay on the plant through the fall and into winter. **Blooms** April to August. **Occurs** throughout much of Utah and the western United States. It is found on benches and uplands in clay soils in mixed desert scrub and pinyon juniper woodlands (5,500 to 8,000 ft)

COMMENTS: It is most commonly found in the central and southern portions of Capitol Reef. Most often seen by visitors around the Visitor Center and along Highway 24 through Fruita. It also occurs in Arches, Bryce Canyon, Canyonlands, Glen Canyon, Grand Staircase, and Zion. There are over 50 varieties of this species in the United States and at least ten varieties in Utah, making this a very complex species.

KAIPAROWITS MILKVETCH

Astragalus malacoides | **Pea Family** Fabaceae

A perennial herb with a thick, woody taproot and short stems. **Stems** are prostrate to slightly ascending, forming a plant between 2" to 10" tall. Compound **leaves** are 1¾" to 5½" long, with 15 to 29 leaflets ⅛" to 1" long and less than ½" wide. Leaflets are oblong to oval, yellow green in color, and covered with stiff, incurved hairs. **Flower** stalks are 1½" to 4½" long with ten to 24 flowers each. The dull, pink purple flowers (⅝" to 1" long) curve upwards at full bloom. Flowers dry to a deep violet color. Oblong **seedpods** may curve up or downwards, are on a short stalk and are covered with stiff hairs. Pods have two chambers. **Blooms** late April to early June. **Occurs** only in southern Utah from the Henry Mountains area south through the Circle Cliffs to the Kaiparowits Plateau. Found on silty clay soils in saltbush scrub, sagebrush, and pinyon juniper woodlands. (5,200 to 7,800 ft)

COMMENTS: This is an endemic species and a National Park Service sensitive species. It is rarely seen but occurs in the southern portions of Capitol Reef, and south to Glen Canyon and Grand Staircase.

WOOLLY MILKVETCH

Astragalus mollissimus | **Pea Family** Fabaceae

A perennial herb 2" to 17" tall. Foliage is densely covered with woolly white hairs, hence the common name. Compound **leaves** are ¾" to 11" long, with 15 to 35 elliptical or egg shaped leaflets that are up to ¾" long. **Flower** stalks extend beyond the leafy branches and have seven to 20 flowers per stalk. The pink purple or bi-colored pink and white flowers curve upwards at full bloom. They are about ½" to 1" long and covered with hairs. **Seedpods** curve downwards, are sessile or nearly so, curved, and up to 1" long and ⅜" wide. They also are densely covered with soft woolly hairs. **Blooms** February to June. **Occurs** throughout Utah and the Southwest, and south into Mexico. Found in many soil types in mixed desert scrub, grasslands, and pinyon juniper communities. (3,700 to 7,600 ft)

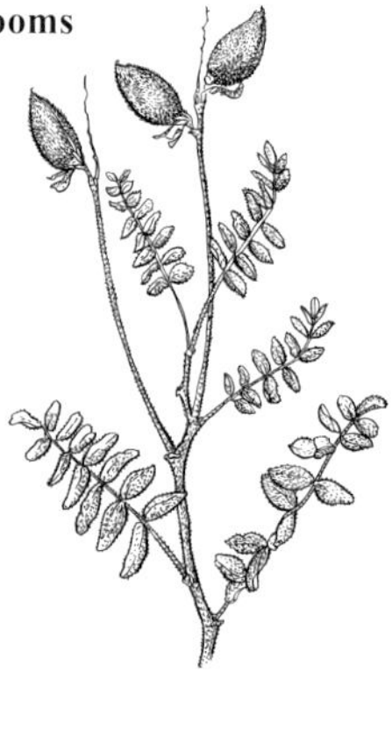

COMMENTS: Commonly seen in the central and southern portions of Capitol Reef. It also occurs in Arches, Canyonlands, Bryce Canyon, Bears Ears, Glen Canyon, Grand Staircase, and Zion. It is one of the first wildflowers to bloom in the spring. This species of milkvetch is highly poisonous to livestock.

FERRON MILKVETCH

Astragalus musiniensis | **Pea Family** Fabaceae

A perennial herb 1" to 5" tall. A small, **stemless** plant covered with short, silvery hairs that give the plant a gray green appearance. Compound **leaves** are ¾" to 5" long with three to five leaflets up to 1⅓" long and are lance shaped to elliptical with acute pointed tips. **Flower** stalks are up to 2¾" long and each stalk has one to six flowers. The pink purple flowers are erect at full bloom. They are only about 1" long, cylinder shaped, and covered with short, stiff hairs. **Seedpods** are ascending and covered with stiff hairs. They are about 1½" long. **Blooms** April to May. **Occurs** only in south central Utah in mixed desert scrub, salt desert, and pinyon juniper woodlands. (4,700 to 7,600 ft)

COMMENTS: Found throughout the lower elevations of Capitol Reef and Canyonlands. It is a fairly common Colorado Plateau endemic species.

WOODRUFF'S MILKVETCH

Astragalus woodruffii | **Pea Family** Fabaceae

A bushy, rush-like perennial up to 22" tall. It often forms a bush as broad as it is tall. Foliage is covered with silvery hairs, giving the plant a gray green appearance. Compound **leaves** are ¾" to 2½" long, with two to nine leaflets up to ¾" long and less than 1/16" wide. Leaflets are rounded at the tip and covered with fine silvery hairs. **Flower** stalks are open and may be up to 7" long, each stalk has eight to 45 flowers. The reddish purple to pink flowers are tinged with white and tip upwards at full bloom. They are about ½" to ¾" long. Flower tube is a short cylindrical shape and covered with fine, soft hairs. **Seedpods** are erect, sessile, oblong, and slightly curved in shape. Pods are about ¾" long and have one chamber. **Blooms** May to June. **Occurs** only in southern Utah. Found on benches in sandy, often seleniferous soils of the Entrada and Summerville formations in mixed desert scrub. (4,300 to 5,500 ft)

COMMENTS: It is an endemic species occasionally found in the central portions of Capitol Reef. Most often seen by visitors along the Notom Road. This species has an unpleasant odor and is an indicator of selenium in the soils.

NORTHERN SWEETVETCH

Hedysarum boreale | **Pea Family** Fabaceae

A moderate sized perennial that grows up to 24" tall as a bushy shrub. **Leaves** are pinnately compound, 1" to 4¾" long, with five to 15 leaflets. Leaflets are about 1⅓" long and ¼" wide, oblong or elliptical in shape. Leaflets may be covered with fine hairs on one or both surfaces, or be smooth without hairs. Floral spikes are up to 6" long, with five to 45 flowers per spike. **Flowers** are pink purple, ½" to 1" long, and ascending. **Seedpods** are flattened and have a striking bi-lobed, spectacle shape. They are yellow green in early development and fade to tan or brownish in maturity. **Blooms** April to August. **Occurs** throughout Utah, north to Canada, and south to Arizona, New Mexico, and Texas. Found in mixed desert scrub, pinyon juniper woodland, and ponderosa pine communities in wash bottoms and uplands. (4,700 to 5,000 ft)

COMMENTS: The seedpods make identification of this genus easy. American Indians reportedly used plants in this genus as food sources. May be seen throughout Capitol Reef, primarily in wash bottoms. It also occurs in Arches, Grand Staircase, Bryce Canyon, Canyonlands, and Glen Canyon.

RYDBERG'S SWEETPEA

Lathyrus brachycalyx | **Pea Family** Fabaceae

A small to medium sized sprawling perennial with erect to horizontal **stems** up to 20" long. Foliage may be woolly with hairs or smooth. **Leaves** are pinnately compound, ¾" to 3½" long, with six to 12 leaflets. Leaflets are about 2" long and up to ⅜" wide, oblong, linear or lance shaped. Twining tendrils occur at the end of each leaf. Floral spikes have two to five flowers per spike. **Flowers** are pink to pink-purple, about 1" long. **Seedpods** are 1" to 1¾" long and up to ¼" wide. **Blooms** late April to June. **Occurs** in southern Utah, Arizona, New Mexico, and Colorado. Found in sandy soils in mixed desert scrub, pinyon juniper woodland, and riparian communities in wash bottoms and uplands. (3,900 to 8,200 ft)

COMMENTS: Found in the southern portions of Capitol Reef. It also occurs in Arches, Canyonlands, Bryce Canyon, Bears Ears, Grand Staircase, and Zion. The genus, *Lathyrus*, comes from the Greek word *lathyros,* which means "pea," hence the common name "sweetpea."

PURPLE LOCOWEED

Oxytropis lambertii | **Pea Family** Fabaceae

An herbaceous perennial with silvery, green leaves, and a taproot that may reach 8' into the ground. Plants are up to 16" tall. Compound **leaves** are basal, 1 1/8" to 12" long, with seven to 17 leaflets to 1¾" long and narrow. Leaflets are oblong to linear, and covered with long, silvery hairs. **Flower** stalks typically are 11" long; each flower spike has eight to 40 flowers. The red purple flowers (⅔" to 1" long) curve upwards at full bloom, with the lower two petals being pointed. Floral bracts are woolly with hairs. Cylindrical **seedpods** curve up at maturity, are sessile, and are covered with hairs. Pods have two chambers. **Blooms** late April to September. **Occurs** in central and southern Utah to Canada and south to New Mexico and Arizona. Found in saltbush scrub, sagebrush, and desert grassland communities. (4,000 to 10,000 ft)

COMMENTS: Most commonly found in the northern portion of Capitol Reef, occasionally seen along the Cathedral Valley Loop Drive. It also occurs in Bryce Canyon and Grand Staircase. Livestock will eat this species when little other forage is available, although it is poisonous. It affects horses most seriously and they may develop a preference for this deadly plant. Some American Indians tribes used this plant to ease constipation and other species of Locoweed were used as food and for medicinal purposes.

Synonyms: Aragallus angustatus, Aragallus aven-nelsonii, Aragallus falcatus, Aragallus involutus, Oxytropis bushii

PURPLE SAGE

Poliomintha incana | **Mint Famil**y Lamiaceae

A moderate sized, erect shrub up to 3' in height, with numerous intricate **branches**. Plant is very aromatic with a pleasant mint odor. Entire shrub (including branches, leaves and flowers) is covered with fine mat-like hairs, giving the plant a dusty white appearance. **Leaves** are opposite and linear to oblong, ⅜" to 1⅛" long. Small pale purple to lavender **flowers** are borne in spikes starting in the upper leaf axils; flowers may have purple dots on the lower petals. **Seeds** are inconspicuous. **Blooms** mid April to September. **Occurs** in central and southern Utah, Nevada, California, Arizona, New Mexico, and east to Texas. Found in sandy soils in washes or stabilized dunes in desert scrub and pinyon juniper woodland. (3,600 to 6,000 ft)

COMMENTS: It is found in the southern portions Capitol Reef; more easily seen along Highway 24 to Goblin Valley, north of Hanksville, Utah. It also occurs in Arches, Canyonlands, Grand Staircase, and Glen Canyon. The Hopi Indians reportedly eat the leaves raw or dried and use the flowers as seasoning in cooking.

Synonyms: Hedeoma incana, Hedeoma incanum

LOW SAND VERBENA

Abronia nana | **Four O'clock Family** Nyctaginaceae

A small perennial herb that typically grows 2" to 6" tall. Base of plant is often covered with brown, dried leaves from previous years' growth. **Leaves** are primarily basal and grow on a short stalk; they are oval to oblong, fleshy, and may be covered with tiny glands. Leaves are up to 1¾" long and ½" wide. Trumpet shaped **flowers** grow in dense terminal clusters at the tips of leafless flower stalks. They are rose to pinkish or white and about 2/3" long. Petals are lobed and flared at the end. **Seeds** are tiny and have five wings. **Blooms** April to May. **Occurs** throughout central and southern Utah to California, Nevada, Arizona, and Colorado. Found in mixed desert scrub and pinyon juniper woodlands in sandy soils. (5,200 to 7,100 ft)

COMMENTS: This species occurs in Capitol Reef, Bryce Canyon, Grand Staircase, and Glen Canyon.

SHOWY FOUR O'CLOCK

Mirabilis multiflora | **Four O'Clock Family** Nyctaginaceae

A large, sprawling perennial that grows up to 36" tall and is usually as broad or broader. **Leaves** grow on a short stalk; they are egg shaped to round, ¾" to 7" long, bright green, and may be pointed at the very tip. Showy magenta **flowers** grow in clusters, and are 1½" to 2½" long and funnel shaped. **Seeds** are about ⅛" in size, hard, dark brown, and round in shape. **Blooms** May to July. **Occurs** in southern and central Utah and many of the western States. Found in mixed desert scrub and pinyon juniper woodland communities. (2,500 to 7,800 ft)

COMMENTS: This species is widespread and common throughout Capitol Reef. It also occurs in Arches, Canyonlands, Glen Canyon, Bears Ears, Grand Staircase, and Zion. Flowers open in the afternoon when touched by full sun, hence the common name. American Indians in the Pueblo Province used this species for a variety of medicinal purposes.

Synonyms: Oxybaphus multiflorus

FOOTHILL OR COMMON INDIAN PAINTBRUSH

Castilleja chromosa | **Broomrape Family** Orobanchaceae

A perennial herb reaching 4" to 22" in height, with the overall appearance of a small, rounded clump. The entire plant is often grayish green in color and covered with fine hairs. Lower **leaves** are generally linear and entire and upper leaves on the stem have three to five lobes. Brilliant red to red-orange **floral bracts** are covered with stiff woolly hairs and each bract has five long, narrow lobes. **Seeds** are inconspicuous. **Blooms** April to June. **Occurs** throughout Utah, Colorado, south to Arizona and New Mexico, west to Oregon, and north to Wyoming and British Columbia. Found in sandy soils on rocky uplands, hills, or benches in sagebrush and pinyon juniper woodlands. (2,000 to 9,100 ft)

COMMENTS: It is common in the central and southern portions of Capitol Reef. This genus was named in honor of the 18th century Spanish botanist, Domingo Castillejo. Indian paintbrushes are root parasitic, meaning they receive some of their nutrients from other plants. To do this, they attach their roots to the roots of other plants (often sagebrush) and take nutrients from their host. It also occurs in Arches, Canyonlands, Bears Ears, Bryce Canyon, and Zion.

Synonyms: Castilleja ewanii, Castilleja martini var. ewanii

LINEARLEAF OR WYOMING INDIAN PAINTBRUSH

Castilleja linariifolia | **Broomrape Family** Orobanchaceae

An herbaceous perennial that grows up to nearly 3' in height. **Stems** are simple or branched, usually without hairs, and yellowish or gray green. They often become purplish later in the season. **Leaves** are 3/8" to 4" long, very narrow and grass like, usually entire, but occasionally lobed and appear to be rolled upward. Bright red to yellow **floral bracts** are mostly three lobed. **Seeds** are inconspicuous. **Blooms** June to October. **Occurs** throughout Utah, Oregon, Nevada, California, north to Montana, Idaho, and Wyoming, and south to Arizona and New Mexico. Found in sandy or clay soils on rocky slopes or mesas in sagebrush or pinyon juniper woodlands. (2,600 to 8,800 ft)

COMMENTS: Common in the central portions of Capitol Reef, and often abundant in CoHab Canyon. It occurs in all the Southern Utah parks and monuments. This is the Wyoming State flower. Indian folklore suggests that the roots of this paintbrush (when boiled) were a remedy for venereal disease.

Synonyms: Castilleja linearis

EASTWOOD'S INDIAN PAINTBRUSH

Castilleja scabrida | **Broomrape Family** Orobanchaceae

An herbaceous perennial that grows up to 9" in height. Numerous **stems** rise from a woody base; stems may be erect or sprawling. They are covered with short spreading hairs that give the foliage an ashy green appearance. **Leaves** are ½" to 1" long, linear and narrow. Upper leaves may be deeply lobed. Bright red to red-orange **floral bracts** are also deeply lobed with the lower ones appearing leaf like. **Seeds** are inconspicuous. **Blooms** April to September. **Occurs** primarily in southern Utah, Colorado, Nevada, and New Mexico. Found in sandy soils in rock crevices, on hills, benches or sandstone domes. (4,400 to 8,400 ft)

COMMENTS: It is found in the central and southern portions of Capitol Reef, but is never abundant. The type locality is in Zion National Park. It also occurs in Canyonlands, Arches, Bears Ears, Grand Staircase, and Glen Canyon.

SCARLET MONKEYFLOWER

Erythranthe eastwoodiae | **Lopseed Family** Phrymaceae

A low growing, sprawling perennial with stout, woody, rounded stems. **Stems** are covered with tiny glands. **Leaves** are borne directly on the stem, opposite, dark green, toothed with sharply pointed tips. They have obvious palmate veining and are up to 2" long, oblong, lance shape, or elliptical. **Flowers** are a deep scarlet color with five pointed lobes, about 1" long. They are unequal in shape, with two lips one larger than the other. **Seed** capsules are elliptical in shape and a bit less than ½" long. **Blooms** May to July. **Occurs** in south central Utah, Arizona, and Colorado. Found in hanging gardens and moist seeps in sandstone canyons. (3,700 to 4,500 ft)

COMMENTS: This Colorado Plateau endemic is found in the southern portion of Capitol Reef, usually reported from Halls Creek area. It also occurs in Arches, Canyonlands, Bears Ears, and Glen Canyon. This species is named for Alice Eastwood, a curator of botany at the California Academy of Sciences in the 1990s.

Synonyms: Mimulus eastwoodiae

EATON'S PENSTEMON

Penstemon eatonii | **Plantago Family** Plantaginaceae

A perennial herb reaching 40" in height, with few to many erect stems. The foliage and **stems** are dark green in color. Basal **leaves** are 1" to 7" long, entire with wavy margins and lance shaped with the attachment at the narrow end. Upper leaves are fewer in number, clasping and smaller in size. Bright red, tubular **flowers** grow in an elongated spike. Each flower is about 1½" long. They hang down or extend outward when in full bloom. **Seeds** are inconspicuous. **Blooms** mid April to July. **Occurs** throughout much of Utah, Nevada, California, Colorado, Arizona, and New Mexico. It typically grows in sandy soils on canyon bottoms, hills, or benches in mixed desert scrub, sagebrush, pinyon juniper woodlands, oak brush, and ponderosa pine communities. (2,800 to 9,700 ft)

COMMENTS: Widespread throughout Capitol Reef and all the Southern Utah parks and monuments. Within Capitol Reef, it is commonly seen in Grand Wash and Capitol Gorge. Hummingbirds pollinate this and many *Penstemon* species. The genus name, *Penstemon*, refers to these plants having five stamens. One of the stamens is bearded, which gave the genus one of its common names, "Beardstongue." A medicinal use for *Penstemons* is using the young plants to make a salve or ointment to treat skin irritations.

UTAH PENSTEMON

Penstemon utahensis | **Plantago Family** Plantaginaceae

A perennial herb 6" to 24" tall, with few to many erect stems. The foliage and **stems** are smooth and gray green in color. **Leaves** are thick, rubbery or flesh to the feel. Basal leaves are ¾" to 4" long, entire and spatula or lance shaped with the attachment at the narrow end. Upper leaves are fewer in number, clasping and smaller in size. Bright iridescent red to red-pink tubular **flowers** grow in an elongated spike. Flowers are ½" to ¾" long, with the lobes opening flat. Flowers extend outward when in full bloom. **Seeds** are inconspicuous. **Blooms** April to June. **Occurs** in central and southern Utah, Nevada, and California. Found in sandy soils on canyon bottoms, hills, or benches in mixed desert scrub, blackbrush, and pinyon juniper woodlands. (4,000 to 8,200 ft)

COMMENTS: Common in the central and southern portions of Capitol Reef, often seen on the hike to Hall's Creek or near Torrey, Utah. Type locality for this species is near Monticello, Utah. It also occurs in Arches, Bryce Canyon, Canyonlands, Bears Ears, Glen Canyon, Grand Staircase, and Zion.

RABBIT VALLEY GILIA

Aliciella caespitosa | **Phlox Family** Polemoniaceae

A long-lived perennial that grows in a cushion like mound. The woody base is covered with persistent dry leaf bases and a basal rosette of leaves. **Stems** are unbranched. Stems and leaves are covered with glands that attract grains of sand. Basal **leaves** are linear, up to ¾" long, very narrow, entire or few lobed, covered with tiny pointed spines. There are few leaves on the stems and these are much reduced in size. Flowering stalks are 1" to 3½" tall. Brilliant red to pink **flowers** are usually solitary, and up to ¾" long, tubular shaped with flaring petal lobes. **Seeds** are inconspicuous. **Blooms** May to July. **Occurs** only in south central Utah. Found in sandy pockets of slickrock chaparral and pinyon juniper woodland. (5,700 to 9,000 ft)

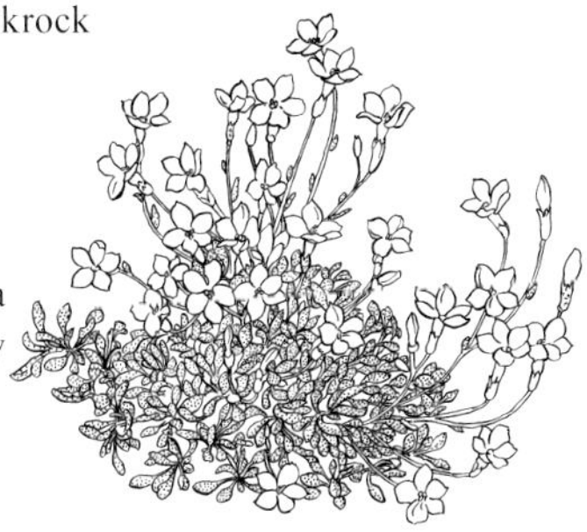

COMMENTS: Until two years ago, this species was a candidate for federal listing. It is still a rare endemic species in need of protection. It is a National Park Service sensitive species currently being monitored in Capitol Reef. Collection of plants and seeds continue to threaten long-term survival of this species.

CANYONLANDS GILIA

Aliciella subnuda | **Phlox Family** Polemoniaceae

A biennial or perennial that grows up to 20" tall. One to a few simple **stems** rise from a basal rosette of leaves. **Leaves** are spatula to egg shaped, variously lobed, and up to 3¾" long. They are densely covered with glandular, sticky hairs that gather sand grains. The carmine to reddish **flowers** are ⅜" to ¾" long, tubular with five flaring lobes, and borne in loose clusters. **Seeds** are inconspicuous. **Blooms** mid April to October. **Occurs** in central and southern Utah, Arizona, New Mexico, and Colorado. Found in sagebrush, mixed desert scrub, pinyon juniper woodland, and ponderosa pine woodland communities. (4,800 to 6,800 ft)

COMMENTS: This showy wildflower is widespread in canyon bottoms, uplands, and benches throughout Capitol Reef, Grand Staircase, and Glen Canyon.

Synonyms: Gilia subnuda

SKYROCKET

Ipomopsis aggregata | **Phlox Family** Polemoniaceae

A biennial or perennial that grows from a basal rosette of leaves. Plants are between 6" and 24" tall. Tall **stems** arise from the center of the rosette. Basal leaves are deeply lobed up to 2" long. **Leaves** on the stem are few, deeply lobed to more than half the distance to the midrib, and reduced upward. The brilliant red to scarlet **flowers** are ¾" to 1½" long, tubular with flared lobes, and borne in loose clusters. **Seeds** are inconspicuous. **Blooms** May to October. **Occurs** throughout Utah, California, Nevada, Arizona, Wyoming, and Colorado. Found in mixed desert scrub, pinyon juniper woodland, ponderosa pine woodlands, and spruce fir communities. (5,000 to 10,600 ft)

COMMENTS: American Indians use this species for a variety of medicinal purposes, including a tonic and treatment for venereal diseases. Occasionally one will find this plant with pink, orange, or white flowers. The specific name, *aggregata*, refers to the clustered arrangement of the flowers. This showy wildflower is widespread throughout Capitol Reef. It also occurs in Zion, Canyonlands, Cedar Breaks, Bears Ears, and Natural Bridges.

SPINY MILKWORT

Polygala subspinosa | **Milkwort Family** Polygalaceae

A small, perennial shrub that forms low rounded clumps often wider than tall. These thorny little plants reach about 8" in height. Spatula or elliptical shaped **leaves** are ⅓" to 1⅓" long and narrow. Bright purple pink **flowers** are borne on short flower stalks. Flowers are about ½" long. **Seeds** are inconspicuous. **Blooms** mid April to July. **Occurs** in central and southern Utah, Nevada, California, New Mexico, Colorado, and Arizona. Found in mixed desert scrub, sagebrush, pinyon juniper woodland, and ponderosa pine communities. (4,300 to 7,500 ft)

COMMENTS: It is found in the central and southern portions of Capitol Reef, most often seen by visitors along the Sulphur Creek walk. It also occurs in Arches, Grand Staircase, and Glen Canyon.

PRETTY BUCKWHEAT

Eriogonum bicolor | **Buckwheat Family** Polygonaceae

An herbaceous perennial that grows as a small rounded mound up to 4" tall. **Stems** tend to grow horizontally along the ground and can be up to 8" broad. All foliage is covered with fine woolly hairs that give the plant a gray green fuzzy appearance. Tiny **leaves** are crowded along the stem internodes, are up to 2/3" long, and very narrow. The lower leaf surface is mostly hidden by the outer margins that are rolled backwards. White (suffused with pink or rose) **flowers** are borne on the ends of very short stalks. Petals' mid-veins have a dark pink or rose stripe. The entire flat-topped flower head is less than 2" across. **Seeds** are inconspicuous. **Blooms** May to June. **Occurs** only in south central Utah. Found in mixed desert scrub, saltbush, sagebrush, and pinyon juniper woodlands. (4,400 to 6,500 ft)

COMMENTS: This is a showy little shrub endemic to southern Utah. Found in the central and southern portions of Capitol Reef; also can be seen just east of the Park along Highway 24. It also occurs in Arches, Canyonlands, and Glen Canyon.

HEIL'S BUCKWHEAT

Eriogonum corymbosum var. heilii | **Buckwheat Family** Polygonaceae

A small, compact sub-shrub approximately 15" broad and reaching to 2' in height (though typically much shorter). **Stems** are angular and ascending. **Leaves** occur on the stems and up to one-fourth of the height of the flowering stem. Leaves are lance shaped to oblong, about ¾" long and ¼" wide, densely hairy on the underside and slightly woolly above. Tiny white to pink **flowers** grow in a terminal flat or slightly rounded cluster. They may be hairy or smooth. Flowers lack petals but have petal like sepals. **Seeds** are inconspicuous. **Blooms** July to August. **Occurs** only in south central Utah. Found in clay soils in sagebrush, pinyon juniper, and Bristlecone pine woodlands. (8,200 to 9,200 ft)

COMMENTS: This variety is endemic to the Thousand Lake Mountain area within and adjacent to Capitol Reef. It is a National Park Service and Forest Service sensitive species.

SLENDER BUCKWHEAT

Eriogonum microthecum | **Buckwheat Family** Polygonaceae

A small, erect shrub easy to miss unless it's in full bloom. **Stems** are angular and ascending. **Leaves** are linear to lance shaped, ⅛" to 1¼" long and may be woolly on the underside with the leaf margins usually rolled under. Tiny **flowers** grow in a flat or slightly rounded cluster; they are white and may be tinged with a pink or rose color. Flowers lack petals but have petal like sepals. **Seeds** are inconspicuous. **Blooms** August to October. **Occurs** throughout much of Utah and the western United States. Found in mixed desert scrub, sagebrush, pinyon juniper, and ponderosa pine woodlands. (3,700 to 9,500 ft)

COMMENTS: Widely distributed and abundant throughout Capitol Reef, and Arches, Bryce Canyon, Canyonlands, Bears Ears, Glen Canyon, Grand Staircase, and Zion.

CUSHION BUCKWHEAT

Eriogonum ovalifolium | **Buckwheat Family** Polygonaceae

An herbaceous perennial that grows as a cushion like mound. The woody base is covered with persistent leaf bases and dried leaves. **Leaves** are basal, ¾" to 2⅜" long and round to spatula shaped. They are covered with fine woolly hairs that give the plant a gray, green fuzzy appearance. The small, white (striped with red) **flowers** are borne in clusters. The showy flower heads appear as small, delicate round balls at the top of each flower stalk. **Seeds** are inconspicuous. **Blooms** mid April to June. **Occurs** throughout Utah, Arizona, California, and New Mexico. Found in mixed desert scrub, shadscale, and pinyon juniper woodlands to alpine meadows. (4,500 to 11,200 ft)

COMMENTS: It is most often found in the central and southern portions of Capitol Reef. There is a yellow flowered phase of this species that also occurs in this area. This species also occurs in Arches, Canyonlands, Bears Ears, Grand Staircase, and Zion.

Synonyms: Eriogonum shockleyi var. packardiae

SHOCKLEY'S BUCKWHEAT

Eriogonum shockleyi | **Buckwheat Family** Polygonaceae

A perennial that grows in a mat or cushion like mound. The woody base is covered with persistent leaf bases and dried leaves. Roots are covered with blackish brown shaggy bark. The tiny **leaves** are ⅛" to ½" long and up to ¼" wide, lance to spatula shaped or elliptical, and covered with fine woolly hairs on both sides that give the plant a gray, green fuzzy appearance. The white to yellow (often suffused with red) **flowers** are borne in little compact balls on the ends of very short stalks or may be sessile amongst the leaves. The entire flower head is about ½" across. **Seeds** are inconspicuous. **Blooms** mid May to July. **Occurs** throughout much of Utah, Idaho, Colorado, California, Arizona, and New Mexico. Found in mixed desert scrub, saltbush, sagebrush, and pinyon juniper woodlands. (4,200 to 6,500 ft)

COMMENTS: It is found throughout Capitol Reef, primarily in heavy clay soils. This tiny shrub is inconspicuous until it is in full bloom. It also occurs in Canyonlands and Glen Canyon.

SAUSAGE LEAF TALINUM

Phemeranthus breviflorus | **Flameflower Family** Talinaceae

A tiny, herbaceous perennial reaching only 2" tall, with stout roots and spreading **branches**. **Leaves** are fleshy and sausage shaped, hence the common name. They grow in clusters around the stem, are about ⅓" long and linear in shape. Delicate, pink to white **flowers** are solitary at the end of flowering stems and about ¾" wide. **Seeds** are inconspicuous. **Blooms** May to June. **Occurs** in south central Utah, Arizona to Texas. Found in sandy soils amongst Navajo and Cedar Mesa sandstone formations in pinyon juniper woodlands. (5,100 to 7,000 ft)

COMMENTS: This tiny plant is often overlooked until it is blooming and one sees a delicate pink flower nestled in the sand. It is found in the central portion of Capitol Reef. It also occurs in Arches, Canyonlands, Grand Staircase, and Bears Ears.

Synonyms: Talinum brachypodium, Talinum brevifolium

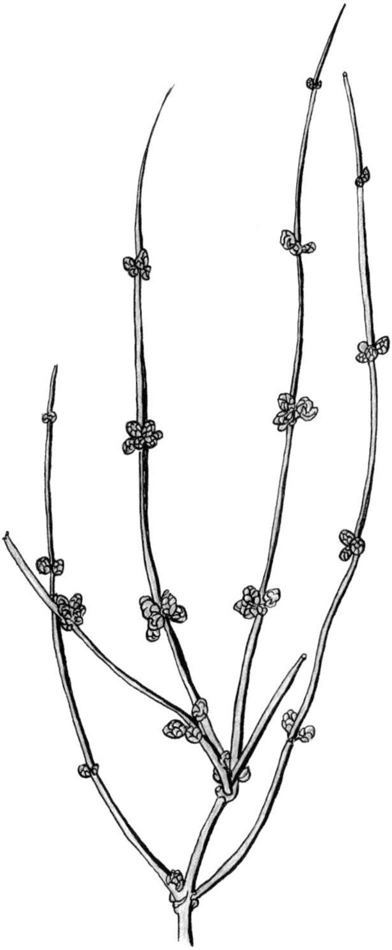

GREEN OR TINY FLOWERS

MATTED SALTBUSH

Atriplex corrugata | **Amaranth Family** Amaranthaceae

A small, mat-forming shrub. **Stems** and leaves are light gray green. **Leaves** are tiny (up to ⅓" long), sessile, and grow alternately along the stem. Very tiny yellow to brownish **flowers** grow in spikes. Tiny **seeds** form within the sessile spike. **Blooms** May to July. **Occurs** in southern and central Utah, Colorado, south to Texas and New Mexico. Typically found in saline, fine textured clay soils and often forms dense monoculture stands of this single species. (4,000 to 8,000 ft)

COMMENTS: Common in clay badlands at lower elevations in the central and southern portions of Capitol Reef, Arches, Grand Staircase, and Glen Canyon.

GARDNER'S SALTBUSH

Atriplex gardneri | **Amaranth Family** Amaranthaceae

A low growing shrub 8" to 20" tall. **Stems** and leaves are grayish green. **Leaves** are small, ½" to 2" long, spatula to oval shaped; they may be sessile or on a short stalk and may grow alternately or opposite along the stem. Very tiny yellow to brownish **flowers** grow in spikes. Tiny **seeds** form within the sessile spike. **Blooms** May to June. **Occurs** in southern and central Utah, Nevada, Colorado, and New Mexico. Typically found in saline, fine textured soils in saltbush and greasewood communities. (4,000 to 7,200 ft)

COMMENTS: This saltbush intergrades with several other species of saltbush and is divided into many varieties making specific varietal identification difficult. It is common in clay badlands at lower elevations in the central and southern portions of Capitol Reef. It also occurs in Arches, Bryce Canyon, Canyonlands, Bears Ears, and Glen Canyon.

Synonyms: Atriplex buxifolia, Atriplex gordonii , Atriplex nuttallii subsp. Buxifolia, Atriplex nuttallii subsp. gardneri, Obione gardneri

HALOGETON

Halogeton glomeratus | **Amaranth Family** Amaranthaceae

A fleshy, annual plant that reaches 20" tall in good conditions, but often found growing only 1" to 3" tall. Alternate **leaves** are ¼" to ¾" long, fleshy with a rounded tip. Leaf tips each have a slender spine that makes the plant prickly to touch, particularly when dry. Small greenish (tinged with pink) **flowers** grow in the leaf axils. **Seeds** are inconspicuous. **Blooms** June to August. **Occurs** throughout Utah and the western United States. Found in disturbed and overgrazed sites in mixed desert scrub communities and along highways where it is introduced in gravel used for paving. It does particularly well in high saline and alkaline soils. (4,000 to 6,500 ft)

COMMENTS: Found throughout the central and southern portions of Capitol Reef in disturbed sites. It also occurs in Arches, Bryce Canyon, Canyonlands, and Glen Canyon. This plant was introduced from Russia into western Nevada in the 1930s as a possible forage crop for livestock. However, it is high in oxalates and is quite toxic to livestock, particularly sheep. It has rapidly spread throughout the desert regions of the western United States and can be a serious threat to livestock.

WINTERFAT

Krascheninnikovia lanata | **Amaranth Family** Amaranthaceae

A moderate sized, erect shrub, up to 30" tall. **Stems** and leaves are gray and woolly with long white hairs. **Leaves** are ⅜" to 1¾" long, alternate, very narrow, linear in shape, and clustered along the stems. Very tiny **flowers** grow in clusters along the stems and are obscured by long, woolly hairs. **Seeds** are white and conspicuously fluffy. **Blooms** May to July. **Occurs** throughout Utah, the western United States, and Canada. Typically found in fine textured soils in saltbush, sagebrush, and pinyon juniper woodlands. (2,400 to 9,300 ft)

COMMENTS: Common in the suitable habitats throughout Capitol Reef. It also occurs in Arches, Canyonlands, Bryce Canyon, Bears Ears, Glen Canyon, Grand Staircase, and Zion. This plant is most commonly noticed in the fall when the long spikes of fluffy fruits wave in the wind. The specific name, *lanata*, means "woolly," referring to the woolly hairs covering the entire plant. It is highly favored forage by deer and bighorn sheep. It is also favored by cattle and disappears quickly in overgrazed areas. American Indians used this plant to treat burns and fevers.

Synonyms: Ceratoides lanata, Eurotia lanata

SKUNKBUSH

Rhus aromatica var. trilobata | **Cashew Family** Anacardiaceae

A moderate sized shrub (up to 8' tall), with numerous irregular branches. Shrubs tend to sprawl nearly as wide as tall and have an unpleasant odor. Old **stems** are grayish, new stems are brownish and very flexible. Compound **leaves** are shiny green on the upper surface and divided into three leaflets. Leaflets are ½" to 1½" long and oval in shape. Leaf margins are slightly lobed or toothed. Tiny yellow flowers are found in dense clusters on short stalks. **Flowers** appear in the spring before the plant leafs out. **Berries** are hard and about the size of small pea, red to red orange, and borne in dense clusters. **Blooms** April to July. **Occurs** throughout Utah, Arizona, New Mexico, Colorado, and south to Texas and Mexico. It typically grows on dry slopes or in washes or canyon bottoms in desert scrub, pinyon juniper woodland, and riparian areas. (2,900 to 7,800 ft)

COMMENTS: It is common and widespread throughout Capitol Reef, often seen in slickrock areas and canyon bottoms. It also occurs in Arches, Bryce Canyon, Canyonlands, Bears Ears, Glen Canyon, Grand Staircase, and Zion. American Indians used the berries to make a lemony-flavored tea drink. American Indian women still use the branches to make baskets and also make dyes from different parts of these plants to color their baskets. The inner part of young twigs makes a yellow dye, leaves and branches make black, and old, fermented berries make a bluish dye. Navajos have several medicinal uses for this species,including a treatment for skin problems, as a contraceptive, to treat stomach problems, and to prevent hair loss.

Synonyms: Rhus trilobata, Schmaltzia trilobata

FRINGED SAGEBRUSH

Artemisia frigida | **Sunflower Family** Asteraceae

A small shrub ranging from 3" to 17" in height. Foliage is gray green in color and soft to the touch. **Stems** may be prostrate or upright in growth and have white, woolly hairs. **Leaves** are also covered with woolly hairs, are up to ¾" in length, and typically are two to three times divided into narrow, linear segments. Flowering stalks extend far above the leafy stems with pale yellow **flowers** growing along the upper portion of the stalk. Flowers are covered with woolly hairs. **Seeds** are inconspicuous. **Blooms** August to September. **Occurs** throughout most of Utah and the western United States to Canada and Alaska. Found in mixed desert scrub, pinyon juniper, and ponderosa pine up to spruce fir and aspen woodlands. (2,900 to 11,500 ft)

COMMENTS: Plants have a pleasant sage scent when you crush the leaves. American Indians have many medicinal uses for this and other sage species. Fringed sage was often made into a tea to help with stomach problems. It is found in the northern portion of Capitol Reef, and in Bryce Canyon, Canyonlands, Bears Ears, Glen Canyon, and Zion.

LONGLEAF BRICKELLBUSH

Brickellia longifolia | **Sunflower Family** Asteraceae

Large, erect shrubs up to 5' tall. **Stems** have white to tan bark. **Leaves** are alternate, borne directly on the stems, are up to 4¾" long, and about ⅓" wide. Leaves are lance shaped with pointed tips. **Flowers** occur in clusters of three to five and are greenish to cream colored. **Seeds** are brown and up to 1" long. **Blooms** September to November. **Occurs** in southern Utah, California, Nevada, and Arizona. Found in riparian areas, canyons, or at springs and seeps. (2,500 to 7,500 ft)

COMMENTS: The genus is named after a botanist, John Brickell, who lived in the southeastern U.S. in the late 18th century. This shrub is found primarily in the southern portion of Capitol Reef, but occasionally in slickrock canyons and moist areas in the central portion as well. It also occurs in Arches, Canyonlands, Bears Ears, Glen Canyon, and Zion.

Synonyms: Coleosanthus longifolius

LITTLE-LEAF BRICKELLBUSH

Brickellia microphylla | **Sunflower Family** Asteraceae

Small, erect shrubs occasionally reaching to 2' in height, more commonly seen about 1' tall. **Stems** have whitish bark; they are erect and almost broom like in appearance. **Leaves** are alternate, tiny, less than ½" long and nearly as wide; they have glands that make them sticky to the touch and may be toothed. **Flowers** are tiny, grow in clusters at the terminal branch ends and are whitish. **Seeds** are tiny fluffs. **Blooms** September to November. **Occurs** throughout Utah, Colorado, Nevada, and Arizona. Found in sandy soils in blackbrush, sagebrush, mixed desert scrub, and pinyon juniper communities. (2,900 to 7,100 ft)

COMMENTS: When crushed, the leaves give off an acrid odor distinctive to all members of this genus. It is widespread throughout Capitol Reef, most often seen by visitors in Grand Wash and Capitol Gorge. It also occurs in Arches, Canyonlands, Bears Ears, Glen Canyon, and Zion.

Synonyms: Bulbostylis microphylla, Coleosanthus microphyllus

MOJAVE BRICKELLBUSH

Brickellia oblongifolia | **Sunflower Family** Asteraceae

A small to moderate sized shrub that reaches 20" in height. **Stems** are green to tan. **Leaves** are alternate, borne directly on the stems, oblong to lance shaped, very glandular, and about 1½" long and ⅝" wide. Leaf edges may be entire or toothed. **Flower heads** are solitary on terminal branch ends, about ¾" long, and covered with tiny glands. **Seeds** are tiny fluffs with blackish tips. **Blooms** September to November. **Occurs** throughout Utah and western United States. Found in blackbrush, mixed desert scrub, pinyon juniper, and ponderosa pine woodlands. (4,200 to 8,200 ft)

COMMENTS: When crushed, the leaves give off an acrid odor distinctive to all members of this genus. It is found in the central and southern portions of Capitol Reef. It also occurs in Arches, Canyonlands, Bryce Canyon, Glen Canyon, Grand Staircase, and Zion.

COPPERWEED

Oxytenia acerosa | **Sunflower Family** Asteraceae

An erect herbaceous perennial that reaches 3' to 5' in height. Plants have long, straight stems that give it a broom-like appearance. Old **stems** near base of plant are gray to brown, while the new growth is greenish. **Leaves** are 1" to 6" long, linear to threadlike, with the margins rolled under. Both stems and leaves are covered with short, stiff hairs. Tiny yellow to cream **flowers** grow on an elongated stalk. **Seeds** are about ¾" long, black and covered with long, shaggy hairs. **Blooms** July to October. **Occurs** throughout much of Utah and the southwestern United States. Found in saline riparian areas, along streams and in seeps and springs. (4,000 to 7,000 ft)

COMMENTS: Found in the central portion of Capitol Reef along the Fremont River, Pleasant Creek, and Spring Canyon, and in the northern portion at springs and seeps, such as Ackland Spring. It also occurs in Arches, Canyonlands, and Bears Ears. This plant has a strong "coppery" or metallic odor when touched. It is poisonous to livestock and can cause a skin rash to some people if they brush against it.

ROUNDLEAF BUFFALOBERRY

Shepherdia rotundifolia | **Oleaster Family** Elaeagnaceae

A large, erect shrub that reaches over 6' in height and is often as wide or wider than tall. Foliage is covered with star shaped hairs. **Leaves** are oval to round, leathery, pale green above and whitish below, and covered with yellow sticky glands. They are about 1½" long and wide. Leaf margins roll under at the edge. Tiny yellow **flowers** grow in clusters in the leaf axils. **Seeds** are berries about ⅓" long. **Blooms** May to July. **Occurs** in southern Utah, Arizona, and Colorado. Found on hillsides, slickrock, and in canyon bottoms in mixed desert scrub and pinyon juniper woodlands. (4,300 to 6,200 ft)

COMMENTS: This Colorado Plateau endemic is widespread throughout Capitol Reef. It also occurs in Bryce Canyon, Canyonlands, Bears Ears, Glen Canyon, Grand Staircase, and Zion. The specific name, *rotundifolia*, refers to the round leaves. Navajos used this plant to soothe sore throats, and ease headaches and toothaches. After touching the foliage of this plant, some people have a reaction similar to that with poison ivy because the stiff, sharp hairs break off in the skin. This genus was named after John Shepard, an English botanist who was a curator of the Liverpool Botanic Gardens during the 18th century.

TORREY'S JOINT FIR

Ephedra torreyana | **Ephedra Family** Ephedraceae

A medium sized shrub that has a scruffy, broom like appearance. **Branches** are grayish green and from a distance, plants appear to have no leaves. In fact, the **leaves** are very tiny (⅛" long), scale like, and grow in the branch joints. Three leaves grow in a whorl around each branch node. The number of leaves per whorl at branch nodes is one of the key differences between Torreys joint fir and Green joint fir. Yellow **flowers** also grow in the nodes around the branch. **Seeds** are in a tiny sessile cone. **Blooms** March to April. **Occurs** in southern and central Utah, Nevada, Colorado, and south to Texas. Typically found on dry sandy ridges in mixed desert scrub, creosote bush scrub, and pinyon juniper woodland. (2,800 to 7,600 ft)

COMMENTS: Common throughout Capitol Reef, particularly in the lower elevation areas of mixed desert scrub. It also occurs in Arches, Canyonlands, Bears Ears, Glen Canyon, and Zion. This genus has been known for its medicinal value for decades. *Ephedra* contains tannins and pseudoephedrines that the Ancestral Puebloan Indians used for tanning hides and for medicinal purposes, such as a cough depressant. The North American *Ephedra* doesn't contain the alkaloid ephedrine used to make antihistamines, but the Old World *Ephedra* from China does. Early pioneers moving west steeped the branches in hot water to make a tea, thus the other common names Mormon or Brigham tea.

GREEN JOINT FIR

Ephedra viridis | **Ephedra Family** Ephedraceae

A medium to large sized shrub that has a broom like appearance. It usually grows much larger than Torrey joint fir. **Branches** are bright green and from a distance, plants appear to have no leaves. In fact, the **leaves** are tiny (⅛" long), scale-like and grow in the branch joints. Two leaves grow in a whorl around each branch node. The number of leaves per whorl at branch nodes is one of the key differences between Torrey joint fir and Green joint fir. Yellow **flowers** grow in the nodes around the branch. **Seeds** are in a tiny sessile cone. **Blooms** March to April. **Occurs** in southern and central Utah, Colorado, Arizona, Nevada, Oregon, and Wyoming. Typically found on dry sandy ridges in mixed desert scrub, sagebrush, and pinyon juniper woodland. It usually grows at slightly higher elevations than does Torrey joint fir. (3,900 to 8,900 ft)

COMMENTS: Found primarily in the central and southern portions of Capitol Reef, particularly in the mid and high elevation ranges. This species occurs in all the Southern Utah parks monuments. A similar species with two leaves per whorl, Nevada joint fir (*Ephedra nevadensis*), occurs west of the Waterpocket Fold and is not bright green.

SINGLELEAF ASH

Fraxinus anomala | **Olive Family** Oleaceae

A shrubby tree that can reach 16', but typically is about half that height. Plants have many slender **stems** that are four-angled. **Leaves** are oval to rounded, fleshy, smooth, dark green above and paler below, about 3⅓" long and nearly as wide. The leaf margins may be entire or slightly serrate. The **flowers** contain no petals, only greenish sepals that grow in dangling clusters. **Seeds** are conspicuous winged fruits similar to that found on maple and other ash trees. **Blooms** April to June. **Occurs** in southern Utah, to Arizona, New Mexico, Colorado, Nevada, and California. Found on hillsides and in canyon bottoms in mixed desert scrub, pinyon juniper woodland, and ponderosa pine communities. (4,300 to 6,200 ft)

COMMENTS: This unusual ash species is found widespread throughout Capitol Reef, and in Arches, Canyonlands, Bears Ears, Glen Canyon, Grand Staircase, and Zion.

BROADLEAF HELLEBORINE

Epipactis gigantea | **Orchid Family** Orchidaceae

An erect, herbaceous perennial, 1' to 4½' tall. **Leaves** clasp the stem and are broadly ovate or oblong near the base of the plant. As leaves ascend the stem, they become more linear (2" to 8" long and ¾" to 2¾" wide). They are bright green in color with obvious parallel veins. Brownish, rose-colored **flowers** grow along the upper part of the **stem**; each showy flower is about ⅔" across with a strongly veined lip often tinged with yellow or rusty red. Lip is three lobed. **Seed** pods are elliptical, up to 1" long and may be slightly hairy. **Blooms** April to July. **Occurs** throughout much of the western U.S. and south into Mexico. Found in hanging gardens, moist seeps, and marshy areas from warm desert scrub to ponderosa pine forests. (3,000 to 8,000 ft)

COMMENTS: An uncommon plant due to its need for dependable moist soils and shady environment. It is found in the very southern portions of Capitol Reef, and in Arches, Canyonlands, Bears Ears, Bryce Canyon, Zion, and Glen Canyon. These plants grow in very fragile locations; do not try to walk right up to them. Enjoy them from a distance so as not to disturb their roots.

Synonyms: Epipactis pringlei ,Serapias gigantean

DESERT TRUMPET

Eriogonum inflatum | **Buckwheat Family** Polygonaceae

An annual or perennial that may grow to 50" tall but is typically only 12" to 18" tall. Plant has one to numerous smooth, greenish, hollow **stems** arising from a basal rosette of leaves. Stems are inflated near the upper joint. **Leaves** are about 1⅛" across with wavy margins; rounded or kidney shaped. Leaf surfaces may be hairy or smooth on one or both surfaces. The tiny yellow or red **flowers** grow in flat or round topped, terminal clusters. **Seeds** are inconspicuous. **Blooms** May to August. **Occurs** throughout much of Utah, to Arizona, Nevada, California, Colorado, New Mexico, and south to Mexico. Found in sandy to clay soils in mixed desert scrub, saltbush, rabbitbrush, grassland, and pinyon juniper woodland communities. (2,500 to 6,500 ft)

COMMENTS: It is common in the central and southern portions of Capitol Reef. It also occurs in Arches, Canyonlands, Bears Ears, Glen Canyon, Grand Staircase, and Zion. The specific name, *inflatum*, refers to the bulbous shape of the upper stem.

WILD RHUBARB

Rumex hymenosepalus | **Buckwheat Family** Polygonaceae

An herbaceous perennial that reaches up to 3 ½' tall and has long, tuberous roots. Lower **leaves** grow on a short stalk are elliptical to lance shaped, up to 10" long, and nearly 5" wide with wavy margins. Leaves on the stems are much reduced in size. All leaves are thick and fleshy. Compact clusters of tiny **flowers** crowd the upper stems, ranging from green to pink to deep rust in color as the flowering season progresses. **Seeds** are oval and have papery, pinkish wings. **Blooms** May to June. **Occurs** in central and southern Utah, and throughout the western United States into Mexico. Found in mixed desert scrub and sandy desert grassland communities, often in disturbed sites. (2,500 to 5,500 ft)

COMMENTS: Found primarily in the southern portion of Capitol Reef. It also occurs in Arches, Canyonlands, Bears Ears, Glen Canyon, Grand Staircase, and Zion. American Indians have used plants in this genus for centuries as a food source, as an antiseptic to treat wounds, and to tan hides. Young leaves, stems, and the roots are all reported to be edible and tasty.

LITTLE-LEAF MOUNTAIN MAHOGANY

Cercocarpus intricatus | **Rose Family** Rosaceae

A moderate to large erect shrub (1½' to 7' tall), with numerous densely packed, intricate branches. **Leaves** are evergreen, ⅛" to ¾" long, narrow, and linear. Leaf margins roll inwards giving leaves a short toothpick like appearance. Very tiny **flowers** lack petals and may be solitary or found in small clusters. **Seeds** have a long showy tail that look like a white plume. **Blooms** April to July. **Occurs** throughout much of Utah, to California, Arizona, and Nevada. Found on dry rocky slopes or in canyon bottoms in desert scrub, pinyon juniper woodland, and ponderosa pine communities. (4,500 to 9,500 ft)

COMMENTS: It is common and widespread throughout Capitol Reef. It also occurs in Arches, Canyonlands, Bears Ears, Glen Canyon, and Zion. This plant is most commonly noticed in the fall when the showy seed plumes mature. The genus name, *Cercocarpus*, comes from the Greek words *kerpos*, meaning "tail," and *carpos*, meaning "fruit."

Synonyms: Cercocarpus ledifolius var intricatus

BASTARD TOADFLAX

Comandra umbellata | **Sandalwood Family** Santalaceae

An herbaceous perennial that grows erect, 3" to 13" tall. Plants may be simple (only one stem) or branching. Alternate **leaves** are pale green, ⅜" to 1¼" long, linear to lance shaped, and smooth. Greenish white **flowers** lack petals, have five sepals, and are borne in terminal clusters. Clusters are about 1" to 1½" across. **Seeds** are inconspicuous. **Blooms** March to August. **Occurs** throughout North America. Found in moist areas in sagebrush, mixed desert scrub, pinyon juniper woodlands, riparian areas, ponderosa pine, and spruce fir communities. (2,800 to 10,400 ft)

COMMENTS: Common in the central and northern portions of Capitol Reef. It also occurs in Arches, Canyonlands, Bears Ears, Bryce Canyon, Glen Canyon, Grand Staircase, and Zion. This species is semiparasitic, and has been recorded parasitizing over 200 species of plants.

CACTUS

ARIZONA SPINYSTAR

Coryphantha vivipara | **Cactus Family** Cactaceae

A small cactus with rounded single or multiple **stems** that reaches 2" to 5" tall. There are 12 to 21 radial spines per areole, which are ⅜" to ⅝" long, and three to 12 central spines of similar length. **Spines** are whitish usually with brownish tips. **Flowers** are bright, shiny, and purple to pink; they are 1" to 2" wide with pointed petals. **Fruits** are oval, about ½" to 1" long, and turn brownish green when ripe. Each fruit contains numerous tiny black seeds. **Blooms** May to July. **Occurs** throughout much of Utah, from Canada to Mexico throughout the western United States. Found in mixed desert scrub, sagebrush, and pinyon juniper woodlands. (2,500 to 8,000 ft)

COMMENTS: A common, beautiful little cactus found in the central and southern portions of Capitol Reef, and in Bryce Canyon, and Zion.

CLARET CUP

Echinocereus triglochidiatus | **Cactus Family** Cactaceae

A medium size cactus that forms a rounded clump with numerous tubular stems. **Stems** are typically 3" to 6" tall and 1½" to 2½" wide, with ribs running vertically along them. **Spines** are stout, white to yellowish, with six to 11 spines per areole. Brilliant scarlet red **flowers** grow from the top of each stem, usually in a small cluster. **Fruit** is small and bright red at maturity. **Blooms** May to June. **Occurs** in southern Utah, Colorado, Arizona, Texas, and New Mexico and into northern Mexico. Found in mixed desert scrub and pinyon juniper woodland communities in sandy to clay soils on upland benches and occasionally in canyon bottoms. (3,200 to 8,400 ft)

COMMENTS: This cactus is showy when blooming and is sure to catch your eye. Found throughout Capitol Reef, and in Arches, Canyonlands, Bears Ears, Bryce Canyon, Glen Canyon, and Zion.

Synonyms: Echinocereus coccineus subsp. mojavensis, Echinocereus triglochidiatus subsp. Triglochidiatus

BRITTLE PRICKLYPEAR

Opuntia fragilis | **Cactus Family** Cactaceae

A small, mat-forming cactus that often spreads out several feet, but only 6" to 8" high. **Stems** are jointed and end in pear shaped pads. Stems are green to greenish blue in color. **Pads** are usually twice as wide as thick, 1" to 2¾" long, and ½" to 1½" wide. **Spines** are straight, whitish, about 1" long with one to eight spines per areole. There may be some white wool around the areoles. **Flowers** vary from yellow to bronze, are about 2¼" across, and grow from the top of each stem. **Fruit** dries to a tan color and may or may not have spines. **Blooms** May to July. **Occurs** throughout Utah, north to Canada and south to Texas, New Mexico, and Arizona. Found in mixed desert scrub, sagebrush, riparian, pinyon juniper woodland, and ponderosa pine communities in sandy soils on uplands, mesa tops, and mountain ridges. (4,500 to 8,400 ft)

COMMENTS: Typically found in the northern and central portions of Capitol Reef; can be seen along the Hickman Bridge Trail. It also occurs in Bryce Canyon and Canyonlands.

PLAINS PRICKLYPEAR

Opuntia polyacantha | **Cactus Family** Cactaceae

A large, mat forming cactus, rarely taller than 6", and often spreading 8' to 10' across. **Stems** are jointed with moderately flattened, oval to circular pads. **Plant** is usually dull green in color. **Pads** are 1½" to 5" long and 1½" to 4" wide and about ½" thick. **Spines** are straight, white to grayish, up to 2" long with one to 15 spines per areole (the upper ones large and stout). Areoles are covered with dense white wool. **Flowers** are 2" to 3" across and vary from yellow to orange to pink with five to ten bright green stigmas in the center. Flowers grow from the top of each stem. **Fruits** dry to a bright red color and are ¾" to 2" long. **Blooms** May to July. **Occurs** throughout Utah, Nevada to Oklahoma and north to Canada. Found in mixed desert scrub, sagebrush, pinyon juniper woodland, and ponderosa pine communities in sandy to rocky soils on uplands, hills, and occasionally in canyon bottoms. (4,500 to 8,400 ft)

COMMENTS: It is common throughout Capitol Reef and particularly showy along the CoHab Canyon Trail in spring. It also occurs in Arches, Canyonlands, Bears Ears, Bryce Canyon, Glen Canyon, Grand Staircase, and Zion.

Synonyms: Opuntia heacockii, Opuntia missouriensis, Opuntia sphaerocarpa

SIMPSON'S PINCUSHION CACTUS

Pediocactus simpsonii | **Cactus Family** Cactaceae

A small cactus that typically grows as a single globe shaped stem. **Stems** are typically 1" to 5" tall and ½" to 8" wide. Numerous short **spines** occur at each areole and cover the entire plant. Spines are white. Cream to pink **flowers** grow clustered at the top of each stem, each about 1" across. Petals have pointed tips and entire edges. **Fruit** turns reddish brown in maturity, is about ¼" long and has few to many triangular shaped scales on it. **Blooms** May to July. **Occurs** throughout most of Utah to Washington, Wyoming, Arizona, New Mexico, and Nevada. Found in mixed desert scrub, pinyon juniper woodland up to Douglas fir communities in sandy to clay soils on upland benches. (4,800 to 9,300 ft)

COMMENTS: Most commonly found in the higher elevations and northern portion of Capitol Reef. It also occurs in Bears Ears and Natural Bridges. There are three closely related *Pediocactus* in the area, two of which are federally listed and protected by law.

Synonyms: Pediocactus hermannii

WINKLER'S PINCUSHION CACTUS

Pediocactus winkleri | **Cactus Family** Cactaceae

Small, usually solitary cacti ranging from ½" to 3" tall and 1" to 3" wide. Tubercles lack central **spines**, and have eight to 14 radial spines. Areoles are persistently white woolly, and elliptic. **Flowers** are ⅔" to 1" long and about as wide, peach to yellowish. Small fruit contain few to many tiny black **seeds**. **Blooms** March to May. **Occurs** only in south central Utah. Found in desert scrub or open pinyon juniper woodland communities. (4,900 to 6,600 ft)

COMMENTS: This species is very rare and is federally listed as threatened. Illegal collection activities threaten the long-term survival of this Colorado Plateau endemic.

Synonyms: Pediocactus bradyi subsp. winkleri, Pediocactus simpsonii var. winkleri

WHIPPLE FISHHOOK CACTUS

Sclerocactus parviflorus | **Cactus Family** Cactaceae

A medium sized cactus that grows as cylindrical stems. **Stems** are typically 2" to 12" tall and 2" to 6" wide, with ribs running vertically along the plant. **Spines** are stout, whitish, with one to four spines per areole; the central one hooked at the end. Clusters of yellow to violet **flowers** (1½" to 2" across) grow from the top of each stem. **Fruit** turns tan in maturity, is about 1" long, and typically has several to numerous triangular shaped scales on it. **Blooms** May to July. **Occurs** in southern and central Utah to Colorado, Arizona, New Mexico, and Nevada. Found in mixed desert scrub to pinyon juniper woodland communities in sandy to clay soils on upland benches and occasionally in canyon bottoms. (4,000 to 8,000 ft)

COMMENTS: Commonly found throughout Capitol Reef. It also occurs in Bears Ears, Canyonlands, Glen Canyon, Arches, and Natural Bridges.

Synonyms: Echinocactus whipplei, Ferocactus parviflorus, Pediocactus parviflorus subsp. intermedius, Pediocactus parviflorus subsp. terrae-canyonae, Pediocactus whipplei

WRIGHT'S FISHHOOK CACTUS

Sclerocactus wrightiae | **Cactus Family** Cactaceae

An egg to short cylindrical shaped cacti ranging from 2" to 5" tall and 1½" to 5" wide. Tubercles are well developed with areoles circular to elliptic. Areoles have one to four central **spines**; the lower one hooked and usually ½" to 1" long. There are eight to 11 radial spines that spread out from the areole. **Flowers** are ¾" to 1⅓" long, are yellowish to white or pinkish, and have magenta filaments bearing the anthers. **Blooms** March to May. **Occurs** only in south central Utah. Found in desert scrub and open pinyon juniper woodland communities. (4,800 to 6,100 ft)

COMMENTS: This Colorado Plateau endemic is federally listed Endangered and is fully protected by the law. Illegal collection activities threaten the long-term survival of this species. It is closely related to *Sclerocactus parviflorus*, also found in Capitol Reef, and may be confused with this common species.

Synonyms: Ferocactus wrightiae, Pediocactus wrightiae

GLOSSARY

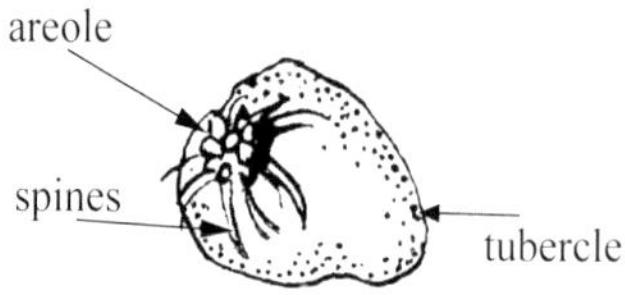

Fig. 1

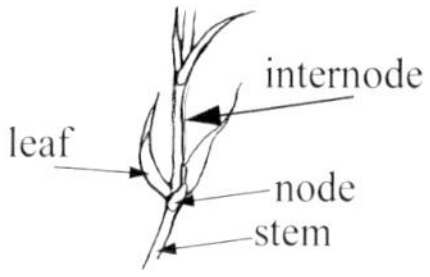

Fig. 6

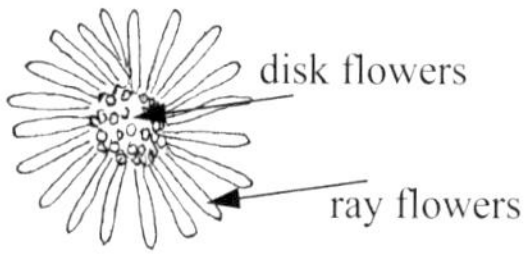

Fig. 2

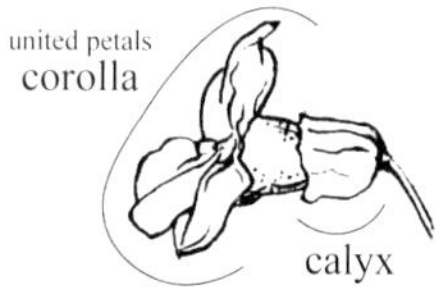

Fig. 7

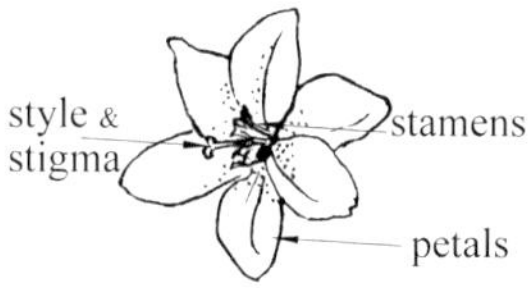

Fig. 3

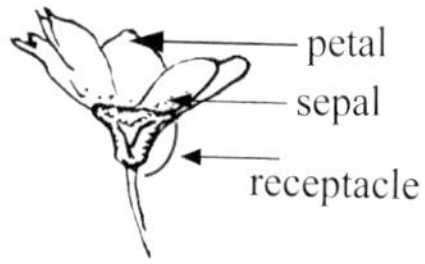

Fig. 8

Fig. 4

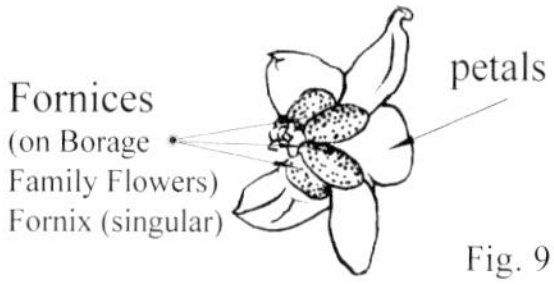

Fig. 9

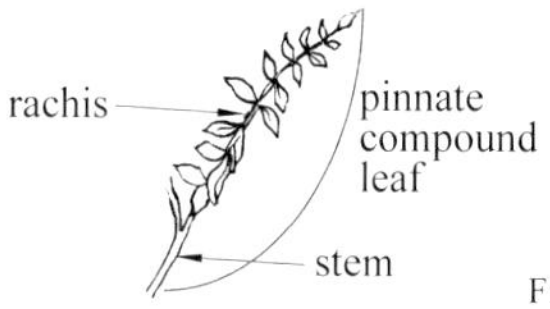

Fig. 5

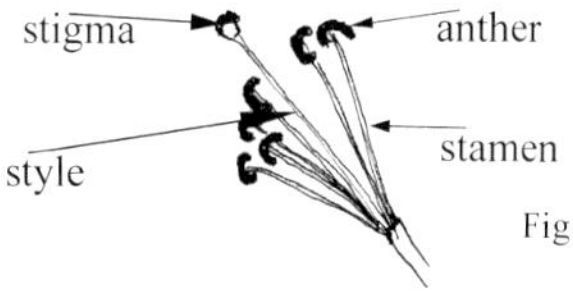

Fig.10

ANTHER
Portion of the stamen that bears the pollen. (See Fig. 10)

AREOLE
Structure on or near the tip of each tubercle on cacti; the structure that bears the spines, flowers, and fruits. (See Fig. 1)

BIENNIAL
A plant that lives two years; typically produces a rosette of leaves or stems the first year, then flowers and sets fruit the second year before dying.

BRACT
A small leaf like structure at the base of flowers; or a much reduced leaf at stem internodes.

CALYX
Term for a set of sepals, the outer whorl below each flower. (See Fig. 7)

COROLLA
Term for a set of petals, the inner whorl of each flower. (See Fig. 7)

DISK FLOWER
Term used for the inner or central set of tubular flowers in each flower cluster in the Sunflower Family (Asteraceae). (See Fig. 2)

DORSI-VENTRALLY COMPRESSED
Refers to the shape of a Pea Family (Fabaceae) seedpod; the side of the pod bearing the seam is flattened; pod is compressed top to bottom.

ENDEMIC
A species that is found only in a limited geographic region and nowhere else.

ENTIRE
Refers to the shape of a leaf with no teeth or lobes.

FORNICES (SINGULAR = FORNIX)
The set of crests at the throat of Borage Family (Boraginaceae) flowers. (See Fig. 9)

HOOD
Outer petal arching above the rest of the flower; found in irregular flowers such as the Milkweed (Asclepiadaceae) and Plantago (Plantaginaceae) families.

INTERNODES
The space between nodes on a stem; nodes are the locations where leaves or spines originate. (See Fig. 6)

LATERALLY COMPRESSED
This refers to the shape of a Pea Family (Fabaceae) seedpod; meaning that the seams for each pod are on the edge; the pod is compressed side to side.

NODE
Point where leaves or branches begin. (See Fig. 6)

PALMATE
Type of leaf shape, leaf lobes are divided from a single point, similar to the shape of a hand with outstretched fingers. (See Fig. 4)

PEDICEL
Stalk of a single flower.

PINNATE
Type of compound leaf shape, leaves have leaflets arranged opposite each other along a single axis. (See Fig. 5)

PISTILS
The female reproductive structures of a flower; typically consists of the stigma, style, and ovary.

RACHIS
Main axis of a compound leaf (supports the leaflets) or flower stalk. (See Fig. 5)

RAY FLOWER
Term used for the outer or surrounding set of flattened flowers in each flower cluster in the Sunflower Family (Asteraceae). (Most people think of these ray flowers as petals.) (See Fig. 2)

RECEPTACLE
The portion of the flower stalk that bears the actual flower parts. (See Fig. 8)

SEPALS
Group of flower structures that form the outer whorl of a flower. Collectively called the calyx. (See Fig. 8)

SESSILE
Attached directly to adjoining flower part, without a stalk. (As in a leaf attached directly to the stem without a stalk)

STAMENS
The male reproductive structures of a flower, consists of the filament and anthers. (See Fig. 10)

STYLE
The portion of pistil that connects the ovary and stigma. (See Figs. 3 & 10)

TUBERCLES
A swelling or protrusion on any structure; cup shaped knobs found on the stem of several cacti species that bear the spines and areoles on or near the tip. (See Fig. 1)

TYPE LOCALITY
Collection location of the specimen for which a species was named.

SELECTED REFERENCES

Bailey, L. H. 1963. *How Plants Get Their Names.* Dover Publications, New York, New York.

Buchanan, H. 1992. *Wildflowers of Southwestern Utah, A Field Guide to Bryce Canyon, Cedar Breaks and Surrounding Plant Communities.* Bryce Canyon Natural History Association, Inc. Distributed by Falcon Press Publishing Co., Helena, Montana.

Carter, Jack L., Martha A. Carter and Donna J. Stevens. 2003. *Common Southwestern Native Plants, An Identification Guide.* Mimbres Publishing, Silver City, New Mexico.

Carter, Jack L. 1997. *Trees and Shrubs of New Mexico.* Johnson Books, Boulder, Colorado.

Coffey, Timothy. 1992. *The History and Folklore of North American Wildflowers.* Facts on File, Inc., New York, New York.

Cronquist, Arthur, et al. 1977 – 2005. *Intermountain Flora, Vascular Plants of the Intermountain West, U.S.A. Volumes 1, 2 Part B, 3 Part A &B, 4, 5, and 6.* New York Botanic Gardens, New York, New York.

Dunmire, William W. and Gail D. Tierney. 1995. *Wild Plants of the Pueblo Province, Exploring Ancient and Enduring Uses.* Museum of New Mexico Press, Santa Fe, New Mexico.

Elmore, Francis H. 1944. *Ethnobotany of the Navajo.* University of New Mexico and School of American Research. University of New Mexico Press.

Elmore, Francis H. 1976. *Shrubs and Trees of the Southwest Uplands.* Southwest Parks and Monuments Association, Tucson, Arizona.

Epple, Anne O. 1995. *A Field Guide to the Plants of Arizona.* LewAnn Publishing Company, Mesa, Arizona.

Fagan, Damian. 1998. *Canyon Country Wildflowers, A Field Guide To Common Wildflowers, Shrubs and Trees.* Falcon publishing, Helena and Billings, Montana.

Harris, James G. and Melinda Woolf Harris. 1994. *Plant Identification Terminology, An Illustrated Glossary.* Spring Lake Publishing, Spring Lake, Utah

Heil, K.D., J.M. Porter, R. Fleming, and W.H. Romme. 1993. *Vascular Flora and Vegetation of Capitol Reef National Park, Utah.* Technical Report NPS/NAUCARE/NRTR-93/01, National Park Service Cooperative Park Studies Unit at Northern Arizona University, Flagstaff, Arizona.

Heil, K.D., S.L. O'Kane, Jr., L. M. Reeves, and A. Clifford. 2013. *Flora of the Four Corners Region: Vascular Plants of the San Juan River Drainage, Arizona, Colorado, New Mexico, and Utah.* Missouri Botanic Gardens Press, St. Louis, Missouri.

Hickman, J.C. (ed.), 1993. *The Jepson Manual.* University of California Press, Berkeley, California.

Intermountainbiota. 2019. Intermountain Region Herbarium Network. HTTP://WWW.INTERMOUNTAINBIOTA.ORG; accessed 3 Oct 2019.

Kearney, T.H. and R.H. Peebles. 1960. *Arizona Flora.* University of California Press, Berkeley, California.

Kindscher, Kelly. 1992. *Medicinal Wild Plants of the Prairie; An Ethnobotanical Guide.* University Press of Kansas, Lawrence, Kansas.

Lesica, Peter and Walter Fertig. 2017. *Spring Wildflowers of Utah's Red Rock Desert.* Trillium Press, Kalispell, Montana.

McMinn, Howard E. 1939. *An Illustrated Manual of California Shrubs.* University Press of California, Berkeley, and Los Angeles, California.

Mayes, V.O. and B.B. Lacy. 1989. *Nanise-A Navajo Herbal, One Hundred Plants from the Navajo Reservation.* Navajo Community College Press, Tsaile, Arizona.

Moore, Michael. 1979. *Medicinal Plants of the Desert and Canyon West.* Museum of New Mexico Press, Santa Fe, New Mexico.

Munz, P.A. 1973. *A California Flora.* University of California Press, Berkeley, California.

National Park Service Species List. HTTP://IRMA.NSP.GOV/NPSECIES/REPORTS/SPECIESLIST

Niehaus, T.F. 1984. *A Field Guide to Southwestern and Texas Wildflowers.* Houghton Mifflin Co., Boston, Massachusetts.

Shaw, Richard J. 1995. *Utah Wildflowers, A Field Guide To The Northern and Central Mountains and Valleys.* Utah State University Press. Logan, Utah.

Stewart, Jon M. 1998. *Mojave Desert Wildflowers, A Field Guide to High Desert Wildflowers of California, Nevada and Arizona.* Jon Stewart Photography, Albuquerque, New Mexico.

Welsh, S.L., N.D. Atwood, S. Goodrich, L.C. Higgins. 2003. *A Utah Flora, Third Edition, revised.* Brigham Young University, Provo, Utah.

Welsh, Stanley L. 1986. *Flowers of the Canyon Country.* University of Utah Press, Salt Lake City, Utah.

Weniger, Del. 1984. *Cacti of Texas and Neighboring States.* University of Texas Press, Austin, Texas.

INDEX

ABOUT THE AUTHOR, PHOTOGRAPHER, AND ARTIST

Deborah Clark, the author, spent twenty years in the Capitol Reef and Bears Ears areas searching for and identifying native plants. For much of that time, she served as the interagency botanist for the Bureau of Land Management, U.S. Forest Service, U.S. Fish and Wildlife Service, and National Park Service. She was the project leader for an interagency rare plant team that conducted surveys within and around Capitol Reef National Park for rare and federally listed plant species. Through this job, she was able to explore much of the backcountry of Capitol Reef and surrounding lands while surveying for rare and endemic plant species.

Thomas Clark, the photographer, worked as the Chief of Cultural and Natural Resources at Capitol Reef for thirteen years before moving on to Canyon de Chelly National Monument, where he worked as the Group Superintendent for Canyon de Chelly and Navajo national monuments, and Hubbell Trading Post. His interest in the diverse natural resources and beautiful landscapes led him to canyon country. His love of the outdoors and photography continues to draw both he and his wife into new places looking for unique plants in the panoramic landscapes of Utah and the southwest.

Patricia Hansen, the artist, lives in Sonoma County, California where she continues her pen and ink artwork in addition to learning new painting techniques. She has a degree in biology and accompanied her biologist husband to assist with fieldwork, do taxidermy on specimens collected, and do detailed drawings of species for publications.

Capitol Reef Natural History Association, a non-profit organization, established to help support Capitol Reef National Park assisted with the design and funding of the first edition of this book.

NOTES

NOTES